Section
504
and the
ADA

To our wonderful wives,
the two Debbies,
With all of our love, always and forever,
Charlie and Allan

Section 504 and the ADA

CHARLES J.
RUSSO

ALLAN G.
OSBORNE, Jr.

CORWIN PRESS

A SAGE Company

For information:

Corwin Press
A SAGE Company
2455 Teller Road
Thousand Oaks,
    California 91320
www.corwinpress.com

SAGE Ltd.
1 Oliver's Yard
55 City Road
London EC1Y 1SP
United Kingdom

SAGE India Pvt. Ltd.
B 1/I 1 Mohan Cooperative
    Industrial Area
Mathura Road, New Delhi 110 044
India

SAGE Asia-Pacific Pte. Ltd.
33 Pekin Street #02-01
Far East Square
Singapore 048763

Printed in the United States of America.

Library of Congress Cataloging-in-Publication Data

Russo, Charles J.
Section 504 and the ADA/Charles J. Russo and Allan G. Osborne, Jr.
      p. cm.
Includes bibliographical references and index.
ISBN 978-1-4129-5508-9 (cloth)
ISBN 978-1-4129-5509-6 (pbk.)
    1. Children with disabilities—Education—Law and legislation—United States.
I. Osborne, Allan G. II. Title.

KF4210.R87 2009
344.73′07911—dc22   2008017844

This book is printed on acid-free paper.

08   09   10   11   12   10   9   8   7   6   5   4   3   2   1

Acquisitions Editor:	Arnis Burvikovs
Associate Editor:	Desirée Enayati
Editorial Assistant:	Irina Dragut
Production Editor:	Cassandra Margaret Seibel
Copy Editor:	Cate Huisman
Typesetter:	C&M Digitals (P) Ltd.
Proofreader:	Susan Schon
Indexer:	Jean Casalegno
Cover Designer:	Rose Storey
Graphic Designer:	Karine Hovsepian

Contents

Preface

SECTION 504 OF THE REHABILITATION ACT OF 1973 AND THE AMERICANS WITH DISABILITIES ACT: IMPLICATIONS FOR EDUCATIONAL LEADERS

Why We Wrote This Book

Americans who are accustomed to living in a world where inequities in schooling and broader society on the basis of race, gender, and disability have largely been eliminated can easily lose sight of what life was like in the not so distant past. For example, in 1969, 15 years after the Supreme Court's monumental decision in *Brown v. Board of Education* (1954) ended state-sanctioned segregation due to race in public schools, Neil Armstrong became the first human to walk on the moon, thereby generating a technological revolution that led to such developments as the Internet, e-mail, and a host of other advancements. Yet, about one-half of American states had laws denying equal educational, and other, opportunities to individuals with disabilities. Even so, change was on the horizon as a result of two cases that were litigated in federal trial courts and that had a profound impact on the rights of individuals with disabilities.

The first case, *Pennsylvania Association for Retarded Children v. Commonwealth of Pennsylvania* (*PARC*) was initiated on behalf of a class of all individuals who were mentally retarded who were excluded from public schools. Ruling in favor of the plaintiffs in *PARC,* a federal trial court held that no child who was mentally retarded or thought to be mentally retarded could be assigned to a special education program or excluded from the public schools without due process. The court added that school systems in Pennsylvania had to provide all children who were mentally retarded with a free appropriate public education and training programs appropriate to their capacities.

The second case, *Mills v. Board of Education of the District of Columbia* (*Mills*), extended the same right to other classes of students with disabilities, establishing the principle that a lack of funds was an insufficient basis for denying these children services. Moreover, *Mills* provided much of the due process language that was later incorporated into the Individuals With Disabilities Education Act (IDEA) and other federal legislation. The court ruled that the board had to expend its available funds equitably so that all students would receive a publicly funded education consistent with their needs and abilities. Additionally, the court directed the board to provide due process safeguards before any children were excluded from the public schools, reassigned, or had their special education services terminated, outlining elaborate due process procedures that it expected the school board to follow.

Insofar as *Mills* was litigated in the nation's capitol, it, like *PARC*, played a major role in congressional reauthorization of a much older federal statute that is actually a labor law, Section 504 of the Rehabilitation Act. Combined with the 1990 Americans With Disabilities Act (ADA), these two laws have had a major impact on students, educators, parents, and all who enter public school facilities but are not covered by the IDEA.

The impact of Section 504 and the ADA dramatically altered the access rights of individuals with disabilities who are otherwise qualified to participate in programs that receive federal financial assistance if they can do so by means of reasonable accommodations and are not subject to defenses that might limit their ability to do so. As far reaching as Section 504 and its regulations are, the latter have still not incorporated "people-first" language into their provisions since they still refer to those who are covered by their protections as "handicapped." Accordingly, while some of the terms used in this book, particularly those referring to judicial statements, may not reflect current language protocols, we have retained their original wording rather than make modifications that might distort the original remarks.

Who Should Read This Book

We are aware of the complexity of Section 504, the ADA, their regulations, and the many cases that they have generated, and this book offers educators wide-ranging information on the rights of individuals who are protected by these two laws. Even so, this book is not intended to serve as a how-to manual. Rather, it is designed to help to make educators aware of the many requirements governing the law as it impacts the rights of individuals with disabilities, in the hope that this increased understanding will put them in a better position to implement both Section 504 and the ADA. In light of the detail that the book provides, it can also serve as a current and concise desk reference for educators ranging from building- or district-level administrators to classroom teachers as well as resource specialists in special education and related fields such as counseling.

Like our other works, this book is not intended to replace the advice and counsel of a school board's attorney. Rather, the book is designed to make practitioners more aware of how the various requirements of Section 504 and the ADA impact the rights of individuals with disabilities in school settings, however broadly construed, in the hope that the educators who understand these laws will be in a better position to meet their myriad legal requirements. We thus caution readers to consult their school board attorneys when difficult situations arise.

This book is organized around the major issues in the law relating to individuals with disabilities. With this organization, the book examines the substantive and procedural requirements that Section 504 and the ADA place on educators. Insofar as there are many issues to cover in a book on special education law, it is a twin challenge selecting both the issues to be grouped in each chapter and the order of the chapters themselves. Based on this challenge, we have organized the chapters in this book around the major procedural and substantive issues affecting the rights of individuals with disabilities. All of the chapters offer recommendations for practice that educational leaders may wish to consider when dealing with Section 504 and the ADA.

Chapter 1 begins with a brief overview of the American legal system by discussing the sources of law. The second section examines the history of the movement to obtain equal educational opportunity rights for students with disabilities, highlighting key cases that shaped the development of Section 504 and eventually the ADA, since developments with regard to the needs of children ultimately impacted on the rights of adults, whether employees, parents, or visitors, in school settings.

The second chapter introduces readers to the specific provisions of Section 504 and the ADA that apply to students, parents, employees, and others who seek the benefits of the programs and services offered by educational institutions. As such, this chapter lays the groundwork for the remainder of the book. After reviewing these materials, the chapter rounds out with a summary and recommendations for educational officials.

Chapter 3, which focuses on legal issues involving students, is divided into three major sections. The first discusses the requirements of Section 504 and the ADA as they apply to students who attend public elementary and secondary schools. The second section presents information on the applicability of the two statutes to nonpublic schools. The third section outlines the laws' requirements with respect to institutions of higher education. Each of these sections analyzes case law to provide guidance as to who qualifies as an individual with a disability, whether individuals are otherwise qualified, and what constitutes reasonable accommodations. The chapter ends with a summary and recommendations for educational officials.

The fourth chapter, which examines issues involving employees, is divided into three substantive sections. These sections address discrimination claims, what it means to be otherwise qualified, and reasonable accommodations. The chapter rounds out with a brief conclusion before offering recommendations for practice. Moreover, in reviewing representative litigation from among the many cases filed pursuant to Section 504 and the ADA, it is important to note that since many of the suits can fit under more than one category because they involve related issues, some of the cases can be found under more than one heading. Insofar as this chapter is concerned with the rights of educational employees with disabilities, it also cites litigation that arose in noneducational contexts, since the implications of these cases apply in educational settings.

Chapter 5 focuses on issues involving parents and the general public. Insofar as educational officials must provide public access to school buildings, property, and programs, this chapter highlights the provisions in Section 504 and the ADA that apply to these two broad constituencies.

The sixth, and final, chapter reviews a variety of topics associated with the options that courts have in evaluating whether discrimination claims against public educational institutions have merit. Among the issues that this chapter addresses are the defenses that educational institutions may rely on, the sovereign immunity of states and state agencies, and damages awards. The chapter also considers whether officials may be sued in their individual capacities, statutes of limitations for filing litigation, and attorney fees awards for successful plaintiffs. Finally, due to the interrelationship of Section 504 and the ADA to the IDEA for students in elementary and secondary schools, the chapter focuses on the requirement that aggrieved parties first pursue remedies under the IDEA before filing suits under Section 504 or the ADA.

The book includes two appendices, one of useful Web sites in education law, the other of Web sites of state departments of education and special education services.

Acknowledgments

We could not have written a book of this nature without the encouragement, support, and assistance of many friends, colleagues, and family members. Thus, while it may be almost impossible to acknowledge all who have influenced us in some way and so contributed to this book, we would at least like to extend our gratitude to those who have had the greatest impact in our lives. This group includes all who have contributed to our knowledge and understanding of the subject matter of this book, most notably our many friends and colleagues who are members of the Education Law Association. These professionals have not only consistently shared their knowledge with us but also, more important, provided constructive criticism and constantly challenged our thinking.

We are also most fortunate to work with a group of professionals who understand the importance of our work and provide us with the support and resources to continue our research. The contributions of many colleagues from the University of Dayton and Quincy Public Schools can never be adequately acknowledged.

In the School of Education and Allied Professions at the University of Dayton, I (Charlie Russo) would like to express my thanks to Rev. Joseph D. Massucci, Chair of the Department of Educational Leadership; Dr. Thomas J. Lasley, Jr., Dean; and Associate Dean Dr. Dan Raisch for their ongoing support and friendship. I also extend a special note of thanks to my assistant Ms. Elizabeth Pearn for her valuable assistance in helping to process the manuscript and Ms. Colleen Wildenhaus for assistance in proofreading the final manuscript and to Mrs. Ann Raney of the Curriculum Materials Center for the many times that she has helped me to find information for this book and many other projects.

I (Allan Osborne) especially thank Superintendent Richard DeCristofaro and the entire administrative team of the Quincy Public Schools for their continuing encouragement and support. In that respect I want to extend a special thank you to my good friend and former colleague, Dennis Carini, whose many questions have helped me to better understand the problems faced by building-level administrators on a daily basis. Most important, I wish to thank a good friend and colleague, Carol Shiffer, Section 504 and ADA coordinator for the Quincy Public Schools, for reviewing and commenting on early drafts of this manuscript. Her input has helped to make this a more user-friendly text.

I would also like to extend a very warm thank you to the faculty, parents, and students of the Snug Harbor Community School in Quincy, Massachusetts, for close to two and a half decades of inspiration. Special thanks are extended to Bob Limoncelli, Chris Karaska, and Amy Carey-Shinney, who provided a wonderful network of support on a daily basis. A school administrator is no better than his or her secretarial staff. I was fortunate to have the best. Much appreciation and love is extended to Angie Priscella and Jeanne Furlong for always being there to make me look good. As this book went to press, I retired from the Quincy Public Schools. As I reflect back on my career as a school administrator I would like to acknowledge that most of my success can be attributed to the wonderful support team behind me.

Finally, I wish to thank two great neighbors, Ed Hacker and Pat Clark, for their friendship and companionship over the past 25 years. My wife and I could not have better neighbors and their constant support and encouragement are very much valued. We look forward to enjoying many more special moments with them.

We would both like to thank our acquisitions editor at Corwin Press, Arnis Burvikovs, and his predecessor, Lizzie Brenkus, for their support as we conceptualized and wrote this book. Thanks also to Cate Huisman, our copy editor, for her typically outstanding efforts. It is a pleasure working with such outstanding professionals and their colleagues at Corwin Press. They certainly helped to make our jobs easier.

On a more personal note, we both extend our appreciation to our late parents, Helen J. and James J. Russo and Allan G. and Ruth L. Osborne. We can never adequately express our gratitude to our parents for the profound influences that they have had on our lives.

I (Charlie Russo) also extend a special note of thanks and appreciation to my two wonderful children, David Peter (and his wife Li Hong) and Emily Rebecca. The two bright and inquisitive children that my wife Debbie and I raised have grown to be wonderful young adults who provide me with a constant source of inspiration and love.

Our wonderful wives, the two Debbies, have been the major influence in our lives and professional careers. Our best friends, they encourage us to write, show great patience as we ramble on endlessly about litigation in special education, and understand when we must spend countless hours working on a manuscript. We would not be able to do all that we do if it were not for their constant love and support. Thus, we dedicate this book to them with all of our love.

C. J. R.

A. G. O.

PUBLISHER'S ACKNOWLEDGMENTS

Corwin Press gratefully acknowledges the contributions of the following individuals:

Kathy Bradberry
Exceptional Needs Specialist
Darlington County School District
Darlington, SC

Dennis R. Dunklee
Associate Professor, Educational Leadership
George Mason University
Fairfax, Virginia

John Enloe
Director of Pupil Personnel Services
Sevier County Board of Education
Sevierville, TN

Mary Guerrette
Director of Special Education
M.S.A.D. #1
Presque Isle, ME

G. Richmond Mancil
Assistant Professor
University of Central Florida
Orlando, FL

About the Authors

Charles J. Russo, JD, EdD, is the Joseph Panzer Chair in Education in the School of Education and Allied Professions and adjunct professor in the school of law at the University of Dayton, Ohio. The 1998–1999 president of the Education Law Association and 2002 winner of its McGhehey (Lifetime Achievement) Award, he is the author of almost 200 articles in peer-reviewed journals and the author, coauthor, editor, or coeditor of 30 books. He has been the editor of the *Yearbook of Education Law* for the Education Law Association since 1995 and has written or coauthored in excess of 650 publications; he is also the editor of two academic journals and serves as a member of more than a dozen editorial boards. He has spoken and taught extensively on issues in education law in the United States and in 21 other nations on all six inhabited continents. In recognition of his work in education law in other countries, he received an honorary PhD from Potchefstroom University, now the Potchefstroom Campus of North-West University, in Potchefstroom, South Africa, in May of 2004.

Allan G. Osborne, Jr., EdD, is the former principal of the Snug Harbor Community School in Quincy, Massachusetts, and an adjunct professor of school law at American International College in Springfield, Massachusetts. He received his doctorate in educational leadership from Boston College. Allan Osborne has authored or coauthored numerous articles, monographs, textbooks, and textbook chapters on special education law, along with textbooks on other aspects of special education. A past president of the Education Law Association (ELA), he has been a frequent presenter at ELA conferences and writes the "Students with Disabilities" chapter of the *Yearbook of Education Law,* which is published by

ELA. Allan Osborne is on the editorial advisory committee of *West's Education Law Reporter* and is coeditor of the "Education Law Into Practice" section of that journal. He also serves as an editorial consultant for many other publications in education law and special education.

1 Introduction

Education and the
American Legal System

KEY CONCEPTS IN THIS CHAPTER

‡ Sources of Law

‡ History of Exclusionary Practices

‡ Effect of the Civil Rights Movement

‡ Equal Educational Opportunity Movement

‡ A New Era for Students With Disabilities

‡ Right to an Appropriate Education

‡ Litigation Leads to New Legislation

INTRODUCTION

A major challenge facing educational leaders is how to address the needs of individuals with disabilities in school settings. While the primary focus of school officials seems to be typically on students, through their parents, it is important to keep in mind that federal and state laws increasingly take into account the need to safeguard the rights of employees and visitors to school facilities.

Students with special needs and their families are covered by the Individuals with Disabilities Education Act (IDEA, 2005), the Americans With Disabilities Act (ADA, 1990), various state laws, and Section 504 of the Rehabilitation Act of 1973 (Section 504, 2005). However, the primary focus of this book is on Section 504 and the ADA, which together with state laws also protect school staff and visitors with disabilities.

As discussed later in this chapter, school officials were not always concerned with the educational needs of students with disabilities. The current focus on the needs of students with disabilities stands in stark contrast to much of American history. Until well into the nineteenth century, most schools in the United States did little or nothing to look after the educational needs of children with special needs. Special schools and classes began to emerge for children who were visually and hearing impaired as well as for those with physical disabilities during the latter half of the nineteenth century; children who had cognitive deficits, emotional problems, or serious physical disabilities were still largely ignored at that time. During this same time, virtually nothing was done to address the needs of school employees or visitors who had disabilities.

> School officials were not always concerned with the educational needs of students with disabilities.

During the late nineteenth and early twentieth centuries, educational reformers developed classes for students who were mentally retarded. Even so, since these programs were segregated, they typically offered little for children with physical disabilities and frequently were taught by personnel who were insufficiently prepared for their jobs. At the same time, federal laws, most notably an earlier iteration of Section 504, began to protect the rights of workers with disabilities who needed vocational rehabilitation and preparation.

Much of the progress that occurred in the early part of the century came grinding to a halt with the onset of the Great Depression. Fortunately, during the latter half, or more precisely, the final third, of the twentieth century, American educational leaders, lawmakers, and others recognized the need to meet the educational concerns of students with disabilities (Scotch, 2001).

When educators and parents think of children with special needs, their thoughts undoubtedly focus on the IDEA, a far-reaching statute that provides a plethora of substantive and procedural safeguards to eligible students and their parents. However, as indicated briefly above, the IDEA is but one of a variety of laws that are designed to protect the rights of individuals with disabilities. Of the other laws, as noted, Section 504 is perhaps the most significant, because it affects not only students and their parents, but also staff, visitors, and anyone else who may have occasion to visit schools. Based on the impact that Section 504 has had on schooling, this book focuses on how it has impacted American education. At the same time, insofar as the key provisions in the ADA are identical to those in Section 504, the book uses cases litigated under the ADA in discussing how these two laws operate.

In light of the framework of statutes, regulations, cases, and other sources of law that protect the rights of students with disabilities, the first of the two sections in this chapter presents a brief overview of the American legal system by discussing the sources of law. Even though some might perceive this material as overly legal, this section is designed to help readers who may be unfamiliar with the general principles of education law so that they may better understand both the following chapters and the legal system within which they operate. The second section examines the history of the movement to obtain equal educational opportunity rights for students with disabilities, highlighting key cases that shaped the development of Section 504, since developments with regard to the needs of children ultimately impacted on the rights of adults, whether employees or visitors, in school settings. The chapter rounds out with recommendations for educational leaders and their governing bodies whether in K–12 or higher education.

SOURCES OF LAW

Constitutions

Simply put, the U.S. Constitution is the supreme law of the land. As the primary source of American law, the Constitution provides the framework within which the entire legal system operates. To this end, all actions taken by the federal and state governments, including state constitutions (which are supreme within their states as long as they do not contradict or limit rights protected under their federal counterpart), statutes, regulations, and common law, are subject to the Constitution as interpreted by the U.S. Supreme Court.

> As the primary source of American law, the Constitution provides the framework within which the entire legal system operates.

As important as education is, it is not mentioned in the federal Constitution. In fact, the earliest federal enactment mentioning education was Article 3 of the Northwest Ordinance of 1787, which declared that "schools and the means of education shall forever be encouraged" (Baron, 1994, p. 86). Pursuant to the Tenth Amendment, according to which "the powers not delegated to the United States by the Constitution, nor prohibited by it to the States, are reserved to the States respectively, or to the people," education is primarily the concern of individual states.

The lack of a direct mention of education in the Constitution notwithstanding, the federal government can intervene in disputes that arise under state law, as in *Brown v. Board of Education* (*Brown,* 1954), if state action denies individuals the rights protected under the Constitution. By way of illustration, in *Brown,* the Supreme Court struck down state-sanctioned racial segregation, because it violated the students' rights to equal protection under the Fourteenth Amendment by denying them equal educational opportunities. In other words, the Justices were able to intervene in what was essentially a dispute under state law, because once states create and open public schools, then the Fourteenth Amendment requires that they be made available to all on an equal basis.

In addition to delineating the rights and responsibilities of Americans, the Constitution creates three coequal branches of government that exist on both the federal and state levels. The legislative, executive, and judicial branches of government, in turn, give rise to the three other sources of law.

Statutes and Regulations

The legislative branch "makes the law." Put another way, once a bill completes the legislative process, it is signed into law by a chief executive, who has the authority to enforce the new statute. Federal statutes are located in the United States Code (U.S.C.) or the United States Code Annotated (U.S.C.A.), a version that is particularly useful for attorneys and other individuals who work with the law, because it provides brief summaries of cases that have interpreted these statutes. State laws are identified by a variety of titles.

Keeping in mind that a statute provides broad directives, the executive branch "enforces" the law by providing details in the form of regulations. For example, a typical compulsory attendance law requires that "except as provided in this section, the parent of a child of compulsory school age shall cause such child to attend a school in the school district in which the child is entitled to attend school" (Ohio Revised Code, § 3321.03 (2001)). Insofar as statutes are typically silent on such matters as curricular content and the length of the school day, these elements are addressed by regulations that are developed by personnel at administrative agencies who are well versed in their areas of expertise. In light of the extent of such regulations, it is safe to say that the professional lives of educators, especially in public schools, are more directly influenced by regulations than by statutes. Federal regulations are located in the Code of Federal Regulations (C.F.R.). State regulations are identified by a variety of titles.

From time to time the U.S. Department of Education, and particularly its Office of Special Education Programs, issues policy letters, typically in response to inquiries from state or local educational officials, to either clarify a regulation or interpret what is required by federal law (Zirkel, 2003). These letters are generally published in the *Federal Register* and are often reproduced by loose-leaf law-reporting services.

Common Law

The fourth and final source of law is judge-made or common law. Common law refers to judicial interpretations of issues, as judges "interpret the law" by examining issues that may have been overlooked in the legislative or regulatory process or that may not have been anticipated when statutes were enacted. In the landmark case of *Marbury v. Madison* (1803), the Supreme Court asserted its authority to review the actions of other branches of American government. Although there is an occasional tension between the three branches of government; the legislative and executive branches generally defer to judicial interpretations of their actions.

Common law is rooted in the concept of precedent, the proposition that a majority ruling of the highest court in a given jurisdiction, or geographic area over which a court has authority, is binding on all lower courts within its jurisdiction. In other words, a ruling of the U.S. Supreme Court is binding throughout the nation, while a decision of a state supreme court is binding only in a given jurisdiction. Persuasive precedent, a ruling from another jurisdiction, is actually not precedent at all. That is, as a court in Massachusetts seeks to resolve a novel legal issue, the judge would typically review precedent from other jurisdictions to determine whether it has been addressed elsewhere. However, since another court is not bound to follow precedent from a different jurisdiction, it remains only persuasive in nature.

Court Systems

The federal courts and most state judicial systems have three levels: trial courts, intermediate appellate courts, and courts of last resort. In federal court, trial courts are known as federal district courts; state trial courts employ a variety of names. Each state has at least one federal district court, and some densely populated states, such as California and New York, have as many as four. Federal intermediate appellate courts are known as circuit courts of appeal; as discussed below, there are 13 circuit courts. State intermediate appellate courts employ a variety of names. The highest court of the land is the U.S. Supreme Court. While most states refer to their high courts as supreme courts, here, too, a variety of titles are in use.

Trial courts typically involve one judge and a jury. The role of the judge, as trier of law, is to apply the law by resolving such issues as the admissibility of evidence and proper instructions for juries on how to apply the law in the disputes under consideration. Federal judges, at all levels, are appointed for life based on the advice and consent of the U.S. Senate. State courts vary, as judges are appointed in some jurisdictions and elected by popular vote in others. Juries function as triers of fact, meaning that they must weigh the versions of events, decide what happened, and enter verdicts based on the evidence presented at trial. As the trier of fact in a special education suit, a jury (or, in a nonjury trial, the judge) reviews the record of administrative, or due process, hearings and additional evidence and hears the testimony of witnesses. In a distinction with a significant difference, parties who lose civil suits are *liable*, while those who are found to be at fault in criminal trials, a matter well beyond the scope of this book, are *guilty*.

Parenthetically, the vast majority of cases involving education are civil litigation. Civil litigation differs from criminal actions in three basic ways. Civil litigation involves private individuals who file claims either against one another or the state on civil matters such as the right to an education; the measure of damages is usually either legal (meaning monetary, to put individuals in the position that they would have been in) or equitable (hoping to have public officials "do the right things" such as making accommodations for a student with a disability under Section 504). The burden of proof is based on a preponderance of the evidence, meaning that a plaintiff must only provide a little more evidence than a defendant, such that the plaintiff would prevail in a civil trial by a jury vote of four-to-two but would lose if it were deadlocked at three. Conversely, in a criminal case, the state must initiate proceedings to punish wrongdoers who have committed an act that violated criminal statutes, the usual punishment is a fine or imprisonment with capital punishment serving as the exception, and the state must prove defendants' guilt by the much higher standard of beyond a reasonable doubt.

Other than a few select areas such as constitutional issues and special education, which is governed by the IDEA, few school-related cases are directly under the jurisdiction of the federal courts. Before disputes can proceed to federal courts, they must generally satisfy one of two broad categories. First, cases must involve diversity of citizenship, namely that the plaintiff and defendant are from two different jurisdictions, and the amount in controversy must be at least $75,000; this latter requirement is imposed because of the high costs associated with operating the federal court system. Second, disputes must involve a federal question, meaning that it must be over the interpretation of the U.S. Constitution, a federal statute, regulation, or crime.

Figure 1.1   Federal Circuit Courts of Appeal

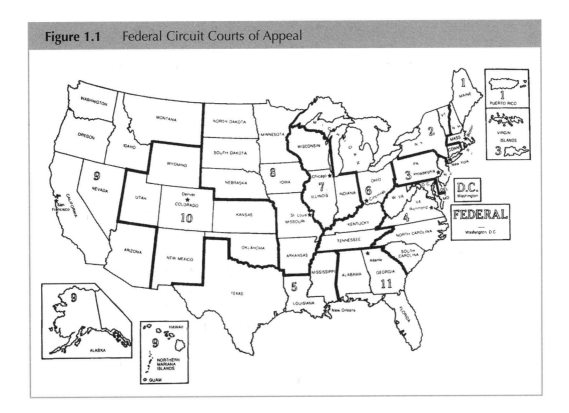

The party that is not satisfied with the decision of a trial court ordinarily has the right to seek discretionary review from an intermediate appellate court. Figure 1.1 illustrates the locations of the 13 federal judicial circuits in the United States. Under this arrangement, which is designed, in part, for administrative ease and convenience, each circuit is composed of several states. By way of illustration, the Sixth Circuit consists of Michigan, Ohio, Kentucky, and Tennessee. State courts with three-tiered systems most often refer to this intermediate appellate level as a court of appeals. Intermediate appellate courts typically consist of three judges and ordinarily review cases for errors in the record of a trial court. This means that appellate panels usually inquire into such matters as whether a trial court judge properly admitted or excluded evidence from trial, not overturning earlier judgments unless such judgments, rather than the facts, are clearly erroneous.

A party not satisfied with the ruling of an intermediate appellate court may seek review from the high court in a jurisdiction. In order for a case to reach the Supreme Court, a party must file a petition seeking a writ of *certiorari* (literally, to be informed). In order to be granted a writ of *certiorari*, at least four of the Court's nine Justices must agree to hear an appeal. Insofar as the Court receives in excess of 7,000 petitions per year and takes, on average, less than 100 cases, it should be clear that few disputes will make their way to the Supreme Court. The denial of a writ of *certiorari* is of no precedential value and merely has the effect of leaving the lower court's decision unchanged. It is generally easier for discretionary appeals in state courts to reach the court of last resort, typically composed of five, seven, or nine members, especially where state law is at issue.

Finding Legal Materials

The opinions of the Justices in Supreme Court cases can be located in a variety of sources. The official version of Supreme Court cases can be found in the *United States Reports* (abbreviated "U.S." in case reference listings). The same text, with additional research aids, are located in the Supreme Court Reporter (S. Ct.) and the Lawyer's Edition, now in its second series (L. Ed.2d). Federal appellate cases are found in the Federal Reporter, now in its third series (F.3d); cases that are not chosen for inclusion in F.3d appear in the Federal Appendix (Fed. Appx). Federal trial court rulings are in the Federal Supplement, now in its second series (F. Supp.2d). State cases are published in a variety of publications, most notably in West's National Reporter system, which breaks the country up into seven regions: Atlantic, North Eastern, North Western, Pacific, South Eastern, South Western, and Southern.

The official versions of federal statutes can be found in the United States Code (U.S.C.) or the unofficial, annotated version published by West, the United States Code Annotated (U.S.C.A.). The final version of federal regulations appears in the Code of Federal Regulations (C.F.R.). As with cases, state statutes and regulations are published in a variety of sources.

Prior to being published in bound volumes, most cases are available in so-called slip opinions from a variety of loose-leaf services and from electronic sources. Statutes and regulations are also available in similar readily accessible formats. Legal materials are also available online from a variety of sources, most notably WestLaw. State laws and regulations are generally available online from each state.

Legal citations are easy to read. The first number indicates the volume number where a case, statute, or regulation is located; the abbreviation refers to the book or series in which the material may be found; the second number indicates the page on which a case begins or the section number of a statute or regulation; the last part of a citation includes the name of the court, for lower court cases, and the year in which the dispute was resolved. For example, the citation for *School Board of Nassau County, Florida v. Arline,* 480 U.S. 273 (1987), the first Supreme Court case applying Section 504 in an educational dispute, affirming that officials violated the rights of a teacher that they had dismissed due to the recurrence of her tuberculosis, indicates that it is located starting on page 273 of volume 480 of the United States Reports. The earlier reported case between the parties, *Arline v. School Board of Nassau County*, 772 F.2d 759 (11th Cir. 1985), which the Eleventh Circuit decided in 1985, begins on page 759 of volume 772 in the Federal Reporter, second series. Following the Supreme Court's ruling, the case was returned to a federal trial court in Florida, *Arline v. School Board of Nassau County*, 692 F. Supp. 1286 (M.D. Fla. 1988), which began on page 1286 of volume 692 of the Federal Supplement; in this opinion, the court held that since the teacher was an otherwise qualified person when she was dismissed, she was entitled to reinstatement and back pay. Similarly, Section 504 of the Rehabilitation Act, 29 U.S.C. § 794(a) (2005) appears at Section 794(a) of Title 29 of the United States Code. Further, Section 504's regulations are published at 34 C.F.R. §§ 104.1 *et seq.* (2000), meaning that they start at part 104.1 of Title 28 of the Code of Federal Regulations.

HISTORY

Exclusionary Practices

In the early years of public education, school programs were usually unavailable to students with disabilities. In fact, the courts frequently sanctioned the exclusion of students with disabilities. For example, in 1893 the Supreme Judicial Court of Massachusetts supported a school committee's exclusion of a student who was mentally retarded (*Watson v. City of Cambridge*, 1893). The student was excluded because he was too "weak minded" to profit from instruction. School records indicated that the student was "troublesome" and was unable to care for himself physically. The court wrote that since the school committee (as school boards in Massachusetts are known) had general charge of the schools, it would not interfere with its judgment. The court explained that if acts of disorder interfered with the operation of the schools, whether committed voluntarily or because of what it described in its own words as imbecility, the school committee should have been able to exclude the offender without being overruled by a jury that lacked expertise in educational matters.

In another dispute, the Supreme Court of Wisconsin upheld the exclusion of a student with a form of paralysis (*State ex rel. Beattie v. Board of Education of Antigo*, 1919). The student had normal intelligence, but his condition caused him to drool and make facial contortions. The student attended public schools through grade five but was excluded thereafter, since school officials claimed that his physical appearance nauseated

> The courts frequently sanctioned the exclusion of students with disabilities.

teachers and other students, his disability required an undue amount of his teacher's time, and he had a negative impact on the discipline and progress of the school. School officials suggested that the student attend a day school for students with hearing impairments and defective speech, but he refused and was supported by his parents. When the board refused to reinstate the student, the court affirmed its decision, maintaining that his right to attend the public schools was not absolute when his presence there was harmful to the best interests of others. The court went so far as to suggest that inasmuch as the student's presence was not in the best interests of the school, the board had an obligation to exclude the student.

An appellate court in Ohio, even in affirming the authority of the state to exclude certain students, recognized the dilemma that was created by exclusionary practices, as they conflicted with compulsory education statutes (*Board of Education of Cleveland Heights v. State ex rel. Goldman*, 1934). At issue was the state's compulsory attendance law, which called for children between the ages of 6 and 18 to attend school. Further, the court decided that the Department of Education had the authority to consider whether certain students were incapable of profiting from instruction. The controversy arose when the board in one community adopted a rule excluding any child with an IQ score below 50, subsequently excluding a student with IQ scores ranging from 45 to 61. In rendering its judgment, the court conceded that the Department of Education could exclude some students. Even so, the court ordered the student's reinstatement, because it was a local board, not the state, that had excluded the child. The court noted that education was so essential that it was compulsory between certain ages.

Civil Rights Movement

The greatest advancements in special education have come since World War II. These advancements have not come easily but resulted from improved professional knowledge, social advancements, and legal mandates initiated by concerned parents, educators, and citizens. The civil rights movement in the United States provided the initial impetus for the efforts to secure educational rights for students with disabilities.

> In *Brown*, the landmark school desegregation case, the Supreme Court unknowingly laid the foundation for future right-to-education cases on behalf of students with disabilities.

In *Brown*, the landmark school desegregation case, the Supreme Court unknowingly laid the foundation for future right-to-education cases on behalf of students with disabilities. Chief Justice Warren, writing for the majority, characterized education as the most important function of government. Warren, pointing out that education was necessary for citizens to exercise their most basic civic responsibilities, explained as follows:

> In these days, it is doubtful that any child may reasonably be expected to succeed in life if he is denied the opportunity of an education. Such an opportunity, where the State has undertaken to provide it, is a right that must be made available to all on equal terms. (*Brown*, 1954, p. 493)

Other courts, dealing with later cases seeking equal educational opportunities for students with disabilities, either directly quoted or paraphrased Warren's comment. As a result, students with disabilities became known as the other minority, as they, largely through their parents and advocacy groups, demanded that they be accorded the same rights to an equal educational opportunity that had been gained by racial and ethnic minorities.

Unfortunately, in the immediate aftermath of *Brown*, the rights of the disabled continued to be overlooked. Throughout the 1950s, more than half of the states had laws calling for the sterilization of individuals with disabilities, while other states limited these individuals' basic rights, such as voting, marrying, and obtaining a driver's license. By the 1960s, the percentage of children with disabilities who were served in public schools began to rise; while 12% of all students with disabilities were in public schools in 1948, the percentage had increased to 21% by 1963 and to 38% by 1968 (Zettel & Ballard, 1982). As of July 1, 1974, the federal Bureau for the Education of the Handicapped reported that about 78.5% of America's 8,150,000 children with disabilities received some form of public education. Of these students, 47.8% received special education and related services, 30.7% received no related services, and the remaining 21.5% received no educational services at all (House Report, 1975).

Equal Educational Opportunity Movement

The movement to procure equal educational opportunities for students with disabilities gained momentum in the late 1960s and early 1970s when parent activists filed suits seeking educational equality for the poor, language minorities, and racial minorities. Although not all of these cases were successful, as with *Brown*, much of the language that emerged from the judicial opinions had direct implications for the cause of students with disabilities.

A New Era for Students With Disabilities

State and federal court cases addressing equal educational opportunities for the poor, language minorities, and racial minorities served as persuasive, rather than binding, precedent in later disputes over access to public school programs for students with disabilities. The legal principles remain the same regardless of why a particular group of students may be classified as a minority. Advocates for students with disabilities successfully used the cases dealing with equal educational opportunities discussed above to lobby for the passage of laws mandating equal treatment for these students.

> Advocates for students with disabilities successfully used the cases dealing with equal educational opportunities discussed above to lobby for the passage of laws mandating equal treatment for these students.

The successes that advocates for students with disabilities enjoyed in mostly lower court cases are considered landmark opinions despite their limited precedential value, since they provided the impetus for Congress to pass sweeping legislation mandating a free appropriate public education for students with disabilities, regardless of the severity or nature of their disabilities. These cases, which are listed by their conceptually related holdings, rather than chronologically, all occurred within a decade of each other and are important because they helped establish many of the legal principles that shaped the far-reaching federal statutes such as Section 504 and the IDEA.

The Right to an Appropriate Education Delineated

One of the first cases that shifted the tide in favor of students with disabilities, *Wolf v. State of Utah* (1969), was filed in a state court on behalf of two children with mental retardation who were denied admission to public schools. As a result, the parents of these children enrolled them in a private day care center at their own expense. As background to the dispute, the parents, through their lawyer, pointed out that according to Utah's state constitution, the public school system should have been open to all children, a provision that the state supreme court interpreted broadly; other state statutes stipulated that all children between the ages of 6 and 21 who had not completed high school were entitled to public education at taxpayers' expense. In light of these provisions, the *Wolf* court, in language that was remarkably similar to portions of *Brown*, declared that children who were mentally retarded were entitled to a free appropriate public education under the state constitution.

Landmark Litigation

Two federal class action suits combined to have a profound impact on the education of students with disabilities. The first case, *Pennsylvania Association for Retarded Children v. Commonwealth of Pennsylvania* (*PARC*, 1971, 1972) was initiated on behalf of a class of all mentally retarded individuals between the ages of 6 and 21 who were excluded from public schools. Commonwealth officials justified the exclusions on the basis of four statutes that relieved them of any obligation to educate children who were certified, in the terminology used at that time, as uneducable and untrainable by school psychologists, allowed officials to postpone school admission to any children who had not attained the mental age of 5 years, excused children who were found unable to profit from education from compulsory attendance, and defined compulsory school age as 8 to 17 while excluding children who were mentally not between those ages. The plaintiff class sought a declaration that the statutes were unconstitutional while also seeking preliminary and permanent injunctions against their enforcement.

PARC was resolved by means of a consent agreement between the parties that was endorsed by a federal trial court. In language that presaged the IDEA, the stipulations maintained that no mentally retarded child, or child thought to be mentally retarded, could be assigned to a special education program or be excluded from the public schools without due process. The consent agreement added that school systems in Pennsylvania had the obligation to provide all mentally retarded children with a free appropriate public education and training programs appropriate to their capacities. Even though *PARC* was a consent decree, thereby arguably limiting its precedential value to the parties, there can be no doubt that it helped to usher in significant positive change with regard to protecting the educational rights of students. *PARC* helped to establish that students who were mentally retarded were entitled to receive a free appropriate public education.

> Two federal class action suits combined to have a profound impact on the education of students with disabilities.

The second case, *Mills v. Board of Education of the District of Columbia* (*Mills*, 1972), extended the same right to other classes of students with disabilities, establishing the principle that a lack of funds was an insufficient basis for denying these children services. Moreover, *Mills* provided much of the due process language that was later incorporated into the IDEA and other federal legislation.

Mills, like *PARC*, was a class action suit brought on behalf of children who were excluded from the public schools in the District of Columbia after they were classified as being behavior problems, mentally retarded, emotionally disturbed, or hyperactive. In fact, in an egregious oversight, the plaintiffs estimated that approximately 18,000 out of 22,000 students with disabilities in the district were not receiving special education services. The plaintiff class sought a declaration of rights and an order directing the school board to provide a publicly supported education to all students with disabilities either within its system of public schools or at alternative programs at public expense. School officials responded that while the board had the responsibility to provide a publicly supported education to meet the needs of all children within its boundaries and that it had failed to do so, it was impossible to afford the plaintiff class the relief it sought due to a lack of funds. Additionally, school personnel admitted that they had not provided the plaintiffs with due process procedures prior to their exclusion.

Entering a judgment on the merits in favor of the plaintiffs, meaning that it went beyond the consent decree in *PARC*, the federal trial court pointed out that the U.S. Constitution, the District of Columbia Code, and its own regulations required the board to provide a publicly supported education to all children, including those with disabilities. The court explained that the board had to expend its available funds equitably so that all students would have received a publicly funded education consistent with their needs and abilities. If sufficient funds were not available, the court asserted that existing funds would have to be distributed in such a manner that no child was entirely excluded and the inadequacies could not be allowed to bear more heavily on one class of students. In so ruling, the court directed the board to provide due process safeguards before any children were excluded from the public schools, reassigned, or had their special education services terminated. At the same time, as part of its opinion, the court outlined elaborate due process procedures that it expected the school board to follow. These procedures later formed the foundation for the due process safeguards that were mandated in the federal special education statute.

Other Significant Cases

Subsequent litigation, although not as high profile as *PARC* and *Mills*, nonetheless helped to establish many of the legal principles that were later incorporated into the federal special education law. In one such case, *In re G. H.* (1974), the Supreme Court of North Dakota maintained that a student with disabilities had a right to an education under the state's constitution. The child's parents moved out of state, leaving her behind at the residential school she had been attending. The school board that had been paying the child's tuition and the welfare department disputed which party was responsible for her educational expenses. The court concluded that the board was liable after acknowledging that the child had the right to have her tuition paid, because special education students were entitled to no less than other pupils under the state constitution. The court suggested that students with disabilities constituted a suspect class, because their disabilities were characteristics that were established solely by the accident of birth. The court reasoned that the deprivation of an equal educational opportunity to a student with disabilities was a denial of equal protection similar to those that had been held to be unconstitutional in racial discrimination cases.

A year after the second judgment in *PARC* and *Mills*, an order of the Family Court of New York City helped establish the principle that special education programs had to be free of all costs to parents. *In re Downey* (1973) was filed on behalf of a student with disabilities who attended an out-of-state school because the city did not have an adequate public facility that could meet his instructional needs. As a result, the child's parents challenged their having to pay the difference between the actual tuition costs and the state aid that they received. The court found that requiring the parents to contribute to the costs of their child's education violated the equal protection clauses of both the federal and state constitutions. In ordering reimbursement for the parents' out-of-pocket expenses, the court was of the view that since children, not their parents, had the right to receive an education, their right should not be limited by their parents' financial situation.

> Subsequent litigation, although not as high profile as *PARC* and *Mills*, nonetheless helped to establish many of the legal principles that were later incorporated into the federal special education law.

In *Fialkowski v. Shapp* (*Shapp*, 1975), another case from Pennsylvania, a federal trial court helped to define what constituted an adequate program for a student with disabilities. Here the parents of two students with severe disabilities claimed that their children were not getting an appropriate education, because they were being taught academic subjects instead of self-help skills. School officials, relying on the Supreme Court's decision in *San Antonio Independent School District v. Rodriguez* (*Rodriguez*, 1973), argued that the claim should have been dismissed, because the children did not have a fundamental right to an education. In *Rodriguez*, the Court held that "education, of course, is not among the rights afforded explicit protection under our Federal Constitution. Nor do we find any basis for saying it is implicitly so protected" (p. 35). Yet, the court responded that *Rodriguez* was not controlling and that the students had not received adequate educations, because their programs were not giving them the tools they would need in life. At the same time, although agreeing with the parents that their children who were mentally retarded could have constituted a suspect class, the court did not find it necessary to consider this question, because it was satisfied that the parents had presented a claim that warranted greater judicial scrutiny than was necessary by the claim of unequal financial expenditures among school systems.

A year after *Shapp*, the same federal trial court in Pennsylvania heard a class action suit filed on behalf of students with specific learning disabilities who allegedly were deprived of an education appropriate to their specialized needs. The complaint in *Frederick L. v. Thomas* (1976, 1977, 1978) charged that students with specific learning disabilities who were not receiving instruction suited to their needs were being discriminated against, while children who did not have disabilities were receiving a free public education appropriate to their needs, mentally retarded children were being provided with a free public education suited to their needs, and some children with specific learning disabilities were receiving special instruction. Therefore, the plaintiffs claimed, students with specific learning disabilities who were not receiving an education designed to overcome their conditions were being denied equal educational opportunities. In refusing to dismiss the claim, the court was convinced that the students did not receive appropriate educational services, in violation of state special education statutes and regulations as well as Section 504 of the Rehabilitation Act of 1973. The Third Circuit agreed that while the trial court's remedial order requiring the local school board to submit a plan identifying all students who were learning disabled was an injunctive order that was subject to further judicial review, the court neither abused its discretion in refusing to abstain nor erred in mandating the identification of all children in the district who had learning disabilities.

A federal trial court in West Virginia, in *Hairston v. Drosick* (1976), established that basic due process safeguards needed to be put in place before a student could be excluded from general education classes. The court held that a local school board violated federal law when officials excluded a minimally disabled student from its public schools without a legitimate educational reason. The student, who had spina bifida, was excluded from general classes even though she was mentally competent to attend school. Further, officials excluded the student even though they did not give her parents any prior written notice or other due process safeguards. The court concluded that the school officials violated the due process clause of the Fourteenth Amendment in excluding the student from general education, placing her in special education without prior written notice, denying her the opportunity to be heard, and failing to meet the requirements of other basic procedural safeguards.

The final groundbreaking lower court case arose in Wisconsin. In *Panitch v. State of Wisconsin* (1977), the federal trial court observed that not providing an appropriate education at public expense to students who were mentally retarded violated the equal protection clause of the Fourteenth Amendment to the U.S. Constitution. Although the state enacted legislation in 1973 that should have provided the relief the plaintiffs sought, by the time the court issued its order four years later, public officials had yet to carry out the law's dictates. Believing that the delay was a sufficient indication of intentional discrimination in violation of the equal protection clause, the court ordered the state to provide the students with appropriate educations at public expense.

Legislative Response to *PARC* and *Mills*

With *PARC* and *Mills* as a backdrop, in 1973 Congress reauthorized a statute that traced its origins to the early twentieth century, when the American economy was beginning its major push to industrialization. Section 504 of the Rehabilitation Act, which is located in the United States Code as a labor law, rather than a statute dealing with education, is part of a lengthy line of legislation that focused on providing vocational rehabilitation for veterans of World War I who were disabled due to their injuries. Following the lead of the federal government, by the early 1920s most states also had vocational rehabilitation services available. Moreover, by 1935 all states offered such services (Scotch, 2001), such that the notion that individuals with disabilities in the workforce were entitled to rehabilitation in order to become productive members of society had deep roots in the American legal system.

Two years after reauthorizing Section 504, Congress passed the most far-reaching special education legislation to date, the Education for All Handicapped Children Act, now known as the IDEA. The IDEA provided funding and a federal mandate for states, and by delegation school systems, to provide all students with disabilities with a free appropriate public education. The IDEA incorporated many of the due process protections for students and their parents first enunciated in the *Mills* decision.

> The enactment of Section 504 set the stage for even more dramatic changes for the disabled with regard to employment, education, and general access to public places.

Approximately 15 years later, Congress added the third major piece of legislation to provide specific rights to individuals with disabilities, the ADA. The ADA extended many of Section 504's protections to the private sector and, at the same time, codified case law that had developed under the latter statute and closed some loopholes. The goal of the ADA, as stated in its preamble, is "to provide a clear and comprehensive national mandate for the elimination of discrimination against individuals with disabilities" (42 U.S.C. § 12101). Even though the ADA is aimed at the private sector, it is still applicable to public entities.

RECOMMENDATIONS

Even though educators wisely rely largely on their attorneys when dealing with technical aspects of disputes involving special education, they should acquaint themselves with both the federal and state legal systems. (Figure 1.2 provides some answers to frequently asked questions about these systems.) By familiarizing themselves with the legal systems of their home states, educators can greatly assist their attorneys and school boards, because such a working knowledge can help to cut right to the heart of issues and help to avoid unnecessary delays. Moreover, educational leaders and their governing bodies in K–12 schools and institutions of higher learning should

- provide regular professional development sessions for all professional staff and board members to help them to have a better understanding of how their legal systems operate and, more specifically, to recognize the significant differences and interplay between and among Section 504, the ADA, the IDEA, and other federal and state disability-related laws so as to better serve the needs of children with disabilities and their parents.
- offer similar informational sessions for parents and qualified students to help ensure that they are aware of their rights.
- develop appropriate handout materials explaining in writing how various federal and state disability laws operate, including detailed information on eligibility criteria under such key statutes as the IDEA, Section 504, and the ADA.
- make sure that all board policies and procedures relating to the delivery of special education and related services are up to date; among the policies that school systems should have in place are those dealing with what materials parents should receive on a regular basis, such as progress reports and report cards for students, notice provisions, and policies calling for parental involvement.
- prepare checklists to help ensure that staff members are responding to parental requests in a timely and appropriate manner.
- determine whether students with disabilities who do not qualify for services under the IDEA require reasonable accommodations under Section 504 and/or the ADA.
- take steps to ensure that students with disabilities are not subjected to differential treatment because of their disabilities or because of their need for accommodations.

- ensure that compliance officers regularly monitor or audit educational programming to make sure that it complies with the dictates of Section 504, the IDEA, and other applicable federal and state laws.
- recognize that in light of the complexity of disability law, it is important to rely on the advice of attorneys who specialize in education law; if school officials are unable to find such attorneys on their own, they should contact their state school board associations, bar associations, or professional groups such as the Education Law Association or National School Boards Association.

Figure 1.2   Frequently Asked Questions

Q. What are the major sources of law that govern public education?

A. There are three major sources of law at both the federal and state levels. The first source is the U.S. Constitution and individual state constitutions. The second source is the statutes enacted by Congress or state legislatures and their implementing regulations (promulgated by the designated federal or state agency). The final source of law is case or common law. This is the body of judicial decisions interpreting the constitutions and statutory provisions as applied to specific situations.

Q. What are the various levels of the court systems?

A. The federal court system has three levels. Most, but not all, state court systems follow this pattern. The lowest level is a trial court. The second level is an intermediate appellate court. Finally, at the top level is the "court of last resort" or a court of final appeals. At the federal level these courts are known respectively as a District Court, a Circuit Court of Appeals, and the United State Supreme Court. As noted, most state court systems have a similar setup, although the names of the courts may be different.

Q. How can I find a statute or a court decision?

A. Federal statutes can be found in the United States Code and federal regulations can be found in the Code of Federal Regulations. State laws and regulations are also found in similar compilations. In the same way, written court opinions can be found in bound volumes such as those in West's National Reporter system. All of these volumes can be located in a law school library or the law library at a courthouse. An excellent source for court decisions in education is *West's Education Law Reporter*, which can be found in the libraries of many colleges that have graduate schools of education. However, most statutes, regulations, and even court opinions can be located on the Internet. Consult the appendix to this book for resources.

Q. Why is it necessary to have laws to protect the rights of individuals with disabilities?

A. The rights of individuals with disabilities have not always been recognized, just as the rights of racial and ethnic minorities have not always been recognized. Unfortunately, the United States has a history of discrimination against and exclusionary practices with regard to individuals with disabilities that required the enactment of civil rights laws to ensure that they were given equal opportunities in areas such as education and employment.

REFERENCES

Americans With Disabilities Act, 42 U.S.C. §§ 12101 *et seq.* (2005).

Arline v. School Board of Nassau County, 772 F.2d 759 (11th Cir. 1985); 692 F. Supp. 1286 (M.D. Fla. 1988).

Baron, R. C. (Ed.). (1994). *Soul of America: Documenting our past, Vol. I: 1492–1870.* Golden, CO: North American Press.

Board of Education of Cleveland Heights v. State ex rel. Goldman, 47 Ohio App. 417 (Ohio Ct. App. 1934).

Brown v. Board of Education, 347 U.S. 483 (1954).

Code of Federal Regulations, as cited.

Downey, In re, 72 Misc.2d 772 (N.Y. Fam. Ct. 1973).

Fialkowski v. Shapp, 405 F. Supp. 946 (E.D. Pa. 1975).

Frederick L. v. Thomas, 408 F. Supp. 832 (E.D. Pa. 1976); 419 F. Supp. 960 (E.D. Pa., 1976); *affirmed*, 557 F.2d 373 (3d Cir. 1977), *appeal after remand*, 578 F.3d 513 (3d Cir. 1978).

G. H., In re, 218 N.W.2d 441 (N.D. 1974).

Hairston v. Drosick, 423 F. Supp. 180 (S.D. W. Va. 1976).

House Report No. 332, 94th Congress (1975).

Individuals With Disabilities Education Act, 20 U.S.C. §§ 1400 *et seq.* (2005).

Marbury v. Madison, 5 U.S. 137 (1803).

Mills v. Board of Education of the District of Columbia, 348 F. Supp. 866 (D.D.C. 1972).

Ohio Revised Code, § 3321.03 (2001).

Panitch v. State of Wisconsin, 444 F. Supp. 320 (E.D. Wis. 1977).

Pennsylvania Association for Retarded Children v. Pennsylvania, 334 F. Supp. 1257 (E.D. Pa. 1971), 343 F. Supp. 279 (E.D. Pa. 1972).

Rehabilitation Act, Section 504, 29 U.S.C. § 794 (1973).

San Antonio Independent School District v. Rodriguez, 411 U.S. 1 (1973).

School Board of Nassau County v. Arline, 480 U.S. 273 (1987); *on remand*, 692 F. Supp. 1286 (M.D. Fla. 1988).

Scotch, R. K. (2001). *From good will to civil rights: Transforming federal disability policy*. Philadelphia, PA: Temple University Press.

State ex rel. Beattie v. Board of Education of Antigo, 169 Wis. 231 (Wis. 1919).

Watson v. City of Cambridge, 157 Mass. 561 (Mass. 1893).

Wolf v. State of Utah, Civ. No. 182646 (Utah Dist. Ct. 1969).

Zettel, J. J., & Ballard, J. (1982). Introduction: Bridging the gap. In J. Ballard, B. A. Ramirez, & F. J. Weintraub (Eds.), *Special education in America: Its legal and governmental foundations* (pp. 1–9). Reston, VA: The Council for Exceptional Children.

Zirkel, P. A. (2003). Do OSEP policy letters have legal weight? *Education Law Reporter, 171*, 391–396.

2 Antidiscrimination Legislation

An Overview of Section 504 of the Rehabilitation Act of 1973 and the Americans With Disabilities Act

---

KEY CONCEPTS IN THIS CHAPTER

✛ Section 504's Provisions

✛ Individual With a Disability Defined

✛ Otherwise Qualified Defined

✛ Provision of Reasonable Accommodations

✛ Application of Section 504 to Others Who Access the School and its Programs

✛ The ADA's Provisions

✛ The ADA's Five Titles

INTRODUCTION

Along with the Individuals with Disabilities Education Act (IDEA, 2005), which is beyond the focus of this book, the rights of persons with disabilities, whether children or adults, are protected by two major federal antidiscrimination laws: Section 504 of the Rehabilitation Act (Section 504, 2005)

and the Americans With Disabilities Act (ADA, 2005). Section 504, enacted in 1973, was the first civil rights legislation that specifically guaranteed the rights of the disabled by prohibiting discrimination in programs or activities that receive federal funds. Section 504's antidiscrimination provisions are similar to those in Titles VI and VII of the Civil Rights Act of 1964 (2005), which forbids employment discrimination in programs that receive federal financial assistance on the basis of race, color, religion, sex, or national origin. Section 504 effectively prohibits discrimination by recipients of federal funds in providing services or employment. In public schools, Section 504 applies to students, employees, and anyone else who desires access to programming, activities, or facilities.

The ADA, signed into law in 1990, prohibits discrimination against individuals with disabilities in the private as well as the public sector. As the ADA's preamble explains, it was designed "to provide a clear and comprehensive national mandate for the elimination of discrimination against individuals with disabilities" (42 U.S.C. § 12101). Essentially, the ADA extends the protections of Section 504 to programs and activities that are not covered by that statute because they do not receive federal funds. Even though the ADA is directed primarily at the private sector, public agencies are subject to some of its provisions. Insofar as the ADA also addressed shortcomings that existed within Section 504, compliance with Section 504 does not automatically translate to compliance with the ADA.

> In public school environments, Section 504 applies to students, employees, and anyone else who desires access to programming, activities, or facilities in educational institutions.

This chapter briefly introduces readers to the provisions of Section 504 and the ADA that apply to students, parents, employees, and others who seek the benefits of the programs and services offered by educational institutions. When thinking of the impact that the ADA and Section 504 can have on schools, both financial and programmatic, New York City's former Mayor Ed Koch's less than complimentary comment on it comes to mind. Koch reportedly stated with some apparent irritation that it would have been easier for New York City to have purchased limousines for all individuals with disabilities than to pay to make its bus system fully accessible (Bricketto, 2003). Analogously, if parents, in particular, were fully aware of the impact of Section 504 and the ADA and the ability of these acts to provide educational programming for their children, then schools would likely be significantly different places. With this in mind, this chapter lays the

> Even though the ADA is directed primarily at the private sector, public agencies are not immune from its provisions.

groundwork for the remainder of the book. After reviewing these materials, the chapter rounds out with a summary and recommendations for educational leaders.

SECTION 504 OF THE REHABILITATION ACT

As noted, Section 504 was the first federal civil rights law protecting the rights of individuals with disabilities. Section 504 provides that "no otherwise qualified individual with a disability in the United States . . . shall, solely by reason of her or his disability, be excluded from the participation in, be denied the benefits of, or be subjected to discrimination under any program or activity receiving Federal financial assistance. . . ." (29 U.S.C. § 794(a)). Section 504 becomes operative when entities receive "federal financial assistance." Thus, Section 504 applies to almost all schools, because this term is interpreted fairly expansively (*Bob Jones University v. United States*, 1983) and offers broad-based protection to individuals under the more nebulous concept of impairment as opposed to disability.

Individual With a Disability Defined

Section 504 defines an individual with a disability as one "who (i) has a physical or mental impairment which substantially limits one or more of such person's major life activities, (ii) has a record of such an impairment, or (iii) is regarded as having such an impairment" (29 U.S.C. § 706(7)(B)). The regulations define physical or mental impairments as including

(A) any physiological disorder or condition, cosmetic disfigurement, or anatomical loss affecting one or more of the following body systems: neurological; musculoskeletal; special sense organs; respiratory, including speech organs; cardiovascular; reproductive, digestive, genito-urinary; hemic and lymphatic; skin; and endocrine; or

(B) any mental or psychological disorder, such as mental retardation, organic brain syndrome, emotional or mental illness, and specific learning disorders. (34 C.F.R. § 104.3(j)(2)(i))

A note accompanying this list indicates that it merely provides examples of the types of impairments that are covered; it is not meant to be exhaustive.

An individual must have a history of, or been identified as having, mental or physical impairments that substantially limit one or more major life activities to be considered to have a record of an impairment. As defined by the Section 504 regulations, individuals who are regarded as having impairments are those who have

(A) a physical or mental impairment that does not substantially limit major life activities but that is treated by a recipient as constituting such a limitation; (B) a physical or mental impairment that substantially limits major life activities only as a result of the attitudes of others toward such impairment; or (C) none of the impairments . . . but is treated by a recipient as having such an impairment. (34 C.F.R. § 104.3(j)(2)(iv))

Major life activities means functions such as caring for one's self, performing manual tasks, walking, seeing, hearing, speaking, breathing, learning, and working. (34 C.F.R. § 104.3(j)(2)(i))

Otherwise Qualified Explained

In addition to having an impairment, an individual must be "otherwise qualified" to receive the protections of Section 504. In the school context a student is "otherwise qualified" when the child is

(i) of an age during which nonhandicapped persons are provided such services,

(ii) of any age during which it is mandatory under state law to provide such services to handicapped persons, or

(iii) [a student] to whom a state is required to provide a free appropriate public education [under the IDEA]. (45 C.F.R. § 84.3(k)(2))

Individuals who are "otherwise qualified," meaning that they are eligible to participate in programs or activities despite the existence of their impairments, must be permitted to take part as long as it is possible to do so by means of "reasonable accommodation[s]" (34 C.F.R. § 104.39).

Once identified, otherwise qualified students are entitled to an appropriate public education, regardless of the nature or severity of their disabilities. Section 504's regulations include due process requirements for evaluation and placement similar to, but not nearly as detailed as, those under the IDEA to guarantee that an appropriate education is made available (34 C.F.R. § 104.36).

Requirement to Provide Reasonable Accommodations

When making accommodations for students with disabilities, school officials must provide aid, benefits, and/or services that are comparable to those available to children who do not have disabilities. This means that otherwise qualified students must have comparable facilities, materials, teacher quality, length of school term, and daily hours of instruction available to them. In addition, programs for students with disabilities should not be separate from those available to other students, unless such segregation is necessary for these students to receive an appropriate education. School boards are not prohibited from providing separate programs for students who have disabilities, but these children cannot be required to attend such classes, unless they cannot be served adequately in more inclusive settings (34 C.F.R. § 104.4(b)(3)). When educational programs are offered separately, facilities must be comparable to those provided to students who do not have disabilities (34 C.F.R. § 104.34(c); *Hendricks v. Gilhool*, 1989).

Otherwise qualified students with disabilities must be provided with reasonable accommodations so that they can participate in a school district's offerings. Reasonable accommodations may involve minor adjustments such as permitting a child to be accompanied to class by a service dog (*Sullivan v. Vallejo City Unified School District*, 1990), modifying a school's behavior policy to accommodate a student who was disruptive due to an illness (*Thomas v. Davidson Academy*, 1994), or providing a sign-language interpreter for a student with a hearing impairment (*Barnes v. Converse College*, 1977). Conversely, school boards do not have to grant all requests for accommodations, particularly if doing so would place an unreasonable burden on boards.

> Otherwise qualified students with disabilities must be provided with reasonable accommodations so that they can participate in a school district's offerings.

Examples of common academic accommodations include giving students longer periods of time to complete assignments or examinations, employing peer tutors, distributing class outlines in advance, allowing children to obtain copies of notes from classmates, using adapted curricular materials, and letting students use computers to take examinations. In adapting facilities, school officials do not have to make every classroom and area of buildings accessible. Generally, it is sufficient to bring services to children. By the same token, it is not necessary to make every building within a school district accessible. School boards may centralize programs for students with disabilities within accessible buildings (*Barnett v. Fairfax County School Board*, 1989, 1991).

At the same time, school boards may not discriminate against employees or job applicants with disabilities. As is the case with students, officials of school boards or other governing bodies (as in higher education) must provide reasonable accommodations for otherwise qualified employees with disabilities. Reasonable accommodations are those that do not place undue financial or administrative burdens on employers or place unreasonable additional requirements on other workers. For example, when employees with disabilities are unable to perform the essential functions of their current positions, employers may be required to reassign them to vacant positions with functions that the employees are able to perform (*Ransom v. State of Arizona Board of Regents,* 1997). However, employers are not required to create new positions or substantially realign the assignments of others in the workplace. Moreover, school board officials cannot be required to reassign custodians who have back injuries to vacant jobs that do not require heavy lifting, nor are they required to reassign duties so that other custodians must do the heavy lifting for their injured colleague.

Application of Section 504 to Parents and Others Who Access a School

Students and employees are not the only persons who may seek access to educational facilities. In the school context, parents frequently need access to buildings and their programs so that they can be active participants in the education of their children. Many public schools also offer educational programs to their communities at large. Section 504 applies when parents and residents wish to participate in school activities (*Rothschild v. Grottenthaler,* 1989, 1990).

AMERICANS WITH DISABILITIES ACT

The Americans With Disabilities Act (42 U.S.C. §§ 12101 *et seq.*), enacted in 1990, protects individuals with disabilities by imposing comprehensive obligations on private sector employers, public services and accommodations, and transportation. As such, the ADA effectively extends the reach of Section 504 to the private sector and programs that do not receive federal financial assistance. The purpose of the ADA, as stated in its preamble, is "to provide a clear and comprehensive national mandate for the elimination of discrimination against individuals with disabilities" (42 U.S.C. § 12101).

ADA's Definition of Individual With a Disability

The ADA provides a sweeping federal mandate for covered entities to eliminate discrimination against individuals with disabilities and to provide "clear, strong, consistent and enforceable standards" (42 U.S.C. § 12101(b)(2)) to help achieve this goal. Comparable to Section 504, the ADA defines an individual with a disability as one who has "(a) a physical or mental impairment that substantially limits one or more of the major life activities; (b) a record of such an impairment; or (c) being regarded as having such an impairment" (42 U.S.C. § 12102(2)). Consistent with Section 504, "major life activities" are defined by the ADA as caring for one's self, hearing, walking, speaking, seeing, breathing, and learning. Neither the ADA nor Section 504 requires that individuals have certificates from doctors or psychologists to be covered by its provisions.

> The ADA effectively extends the reach of Section 504 to the private sector and programs that do not receive federal financial assistance.

Exceptions

The ADA specifically excludes a variety of individuals from its protections. Most notably are those who use illegal drugs (42 U.S.C. § 12210), but the ADA also specifically excludes transvestites (42 U.S.C. § 12208); homosexuals and bisexuals (42 U.S.C. § 12211(a)); transsexuals, pedophiles, exhibitionists, voyeurs, and those with sexual behavior disorders (42 U.S.C. § 12211(b)); and those with conditions such as psychoactive substance use disorders stemming from current illegal use of drugs (42 U.S.C. § 12211(c)). Additionally, the ADA modifies Section 504 insofar as it covers individuals who are no longer engaged in illegal drug use, including those who have successfully completed drug treatment or have otherwise been rehabilitated and those who have been "erroneously" regarded as being drug users (42 U.S.C. § 12110).

Five Titles of the ADA

The ADA has five major parts known as Titles. Title I covers employment in the private sector and is directly applicable to private schools. This Title requires school officials to make reasonable accommodations for otherwise qualified individuals once personnel are aware of the individuals' conditions. This means that in order to be covered by the ADA, students and staff need to inform school officials of their conditions and to provide specific suggestions on how their needs can be met. Title II applies to the public services of state and local governments for both employers and providers, including transportation and especially education, because part of this Title applies to public schools.

Title III is concerned with public accommodations. By covering both the private and public sectors this Title expands the scope of Section 504. Title III includes private businesses and a wide array of community services, including buildings, transportation systems, parks, recreational facilities, hotels, and theaters. Title IV addresses telecommunications, specifically voice and nonvoice systems.

Title V contains the ADA's miscellaneous provisions. These parts of the law maintain both that the ADA cannot be construed as applying a lesser standard than would be applied under Section 504 and its regulations and that qualified individuals are not required to accept services that fall short of meeting their needs.

Similarities Between Section 504 and the ADA

The ADA's impact on students is most significant in the area of reasonable accommodations in academic programs. While schools are subject to many ADA-like regulations under Section 504, compliance with the latter act should ensure compliance with the former. In other words, if school systems have faithfully implemented Section 504 and its regulations, they should not have difficulties with the ADA. School board officials can avoid difficulties with the ADA by implementing proactive policies and procedures to provide reasonable accommodations when needed. Similarly, regarding employees, the ADA's greatest impact is on providing reasonable accommodations for otherwise qualified individuals. Again, in public educational settings, compliance with Section 504 in this respect generally translates to compliance with the ADA.

SUMMARY

Section 504 and the ADA together prohibit discrimination against individuals with disabilities in most educational institutions. Under these laws, persons with impairments that adversely affect major life activities are considered to be individuals with disabilities. In order to be protected by Section 504 and the ADA, individuals must be otherwise qualified to participate in institutions' programs and services. For the most part, being otherwise qualified means that persons can meet minimum programmatic requirements and can participate in activities or benefits despite the fact that they have impairments.

Educational institutions must provide reasonable accommodations if doing so allows individuals with disabilities to access or participate in their programs and services. Generally speaking, accommodations are not reasonable when they place undue financial or administrative burdens on the institutions or result in health or safety risks to individuals with disabilities or others. Thus, accommodations that are excessively costly or that infringe on the rights of others are generally not required. Figure 2.1 provides some answers to frequently asked questions about antidiscrimination legislation.

RECOMMENDATIONS

School boards and educational leaders should

- make sure that qualified individuals, whether students, staff, parents, or guests with disabilities, are not excluded from educational institutions or denied access to programs, benefits, or services solely because of their disabilities.
- ascertain whether individuals with disabilities can meet the minimum requirements for programs if provided with reasonable accommodations.
- not subject individuals with disabilities to differential treatment solely because of their disabilities or because they receive accommodations.
- consider whether requested accommodations would create undue financial or administrative burdens; if they do, consider whether these burdens can be overcome.
- make individualized inquiries into a situation before making decisions regarding reasonable accommodations.

Figure 2.1   Frequently Asked Questions

Q. What constitutes disabilities under Section 504 and the ADA?

A. Disabilities under Section 504 and the ADA are impairments that substantially limit individuals in one or more major life activities. In addition, an individual must have a record of impairments or must be regarded as having impairments. Impairments may be either physical or mental and should be permanent or long term. Within the school context, both learning and working constitute major life activities.

(Continued)

Figure 2.1 (Continued)

Q. What are major life activities?

A. Although this list is not exhaustive, major life activities include such everyday functions as caring for oneself, performing manual tasks, walking, seeing, hearing, speaking, breathing, learning, and working.

Q. When are individuals with disabilities otherwise qualified?

A. Individuals with disabilities are otherwise qualified if they can perform the essential functions of positions with reasonable accommodations in spite of their disabilities.

Q. When are requested accommodations unreasonable?

A. Answers to this question are case specific, requiring individualized inquiries into the circumstances. In general, requested accommodations are unreasonable if they create excessive financial burdens on entities, require educational institutions to alter their missions significantly, create health or safety risks for those who request them or others, or create undue administrative burdens. What is reasonable under some circumstances may be unreasonable in others.

Q. What are essential functions of a position?

A. Essential functions are those aspects of positions that individuals must carry out as part of their jobs. For example, numerous courts agreed that the ability to be physically present in the workplace is an essential function of most positions. On the other hand, being able to answer a telephone may not be an essential function of a clerical position if it is only a small part of an overall job and others in the office could easily take on that task.

REFERENCES

Americans With Disabilities Act, 42 U.S.C. §§ 12101 *et seq.* (2005).

Barnes v. Converse College, 436 F. Supp. (D.S.C. 1977).

Barnett v. Fairfax County School Board, 721 F. Supp. 757 (E.D. Va. 1989), *affirmed,* 927 F.2d 146 (4th Cir. 1991).

Bob Jones University v. United States, 461 U.S. 574 (1983).

Bricketto, M. (2003, April 21). Transportation as civil rights for the disabled. *Gotham Gazette.* Retrieved January 2, 2008, from http://www.gothamgazette .com/article//20030421/202/355

Civil Rights Act of 1964, 42 U.S.C. §§ 2000 *et seq.* (2005).

Hendricks v. Gilhool, 709 F. Supp. 1362 (E.D. Pa. 1989).

Individuals with Disabilities Education Act, 20 U.S.C. §§ 1400 *et seq.* (2005).

Ransom v. State of Arizona Board of Regents, 983 F. Supp. 895 (D. Ariz. 1997).

Rehabilitation Act, Section 504, 29 U.S.C. § 794 (2005).

Rothschild v. Grottenthaler, 716 F. Supp. 796 (S.D.N.Y. 1989), 725 F. Supp. 776 (S.D.N.Y. 1989), *affirmed in part, vacated and remanded in part* 907 F.2d 286 (2d Cir. 1990).

Sullivan v. Vallejo City Unified School District, 731 F. Supp. 947 (E.D. Cal. 1990).

Thomas v. Davidson Academy, 846 F. Supp. 611 (M.D. Tenn. 1994).

3 Students

INTRODUCTION

Students with disabilities in the public schools of the United States are entitled to receive an appropriate education. This entitlement is spelled out in four federal statutes: the No Child Left Behind Act (NCLB, 2002), the Individuals with Disabilities Education Act (IDEA, 2005), Section 504 of the Rehabilitation Act (Section 504, 2005), and the Americans With Disabilities Act (ADA, 2005). Insofar as this book is concerned with the latter two statutes, this chapter focuses on students' rights to services under Section 504 and the ADA.

Both Section 504 and the ADA cover students regardless of their levels of education or ages. While students in elementary and secondary schools may be covered by all four of the statutes identified in the previous paragraph, those in postsecondary institutions are protected by the provisions of Section 504 and the ADA only. As such, students are entitled to protection from discrimination and to reasonable accommodations that allow them to access a school's programs and services. To the extent that many colleges, universities, and other institutions of higher learning receive federal funds in some form, they are subject to Section 504's mandates. The ADA generally covers even those institutions that do not receive federal funds.

As indicated in Chapter 2, both Section 504 and the ADA prohibit discrimination against students with disabilities. Pursuant to these two statutes, officials in schools or other educational institutions must provide reasonable accommodations for otherwise qualified students with disabilities. Students are otherwise qualified if they are eligible to participate in programs or activities in spite of their impairments. Students with disabilities at the elementary and secondary levels are entitled to an appropriate public education, regardless of the nature or severity of their disabilities.

> Both Section 504 and the ADA prohibit discrimination against students with disabilities.

Officials in schools and other educational facilities must provide otherwise qualified students with disabilities with reasonable accommodations so they can participate in educational and other programming, such as sports. In schools, most accommodations allow students with disabilities to access academic programs. In this way, educational officials might make provisions for students to be given more time to complete assignments or examinations, provide adapted curricular materials, or otherwise modify the environment so that individuals with disabilities have full access.

This chapter is divided into three major sections. The first part discusses the requirements of Section 504 and the ADA as they apply to students who attend public elementary and secondary schools. The second section presents information on the applicability of Section 504 and the ADA to nonpublic schools. The third part outlines the requirements that Section 504 and the ADA place on institutions of higher education. Each of these sections includes an analysis of case law to provide additional guidance as to who qualifies as an individual with disabilities, whether individuals are otherwise qualified, and what constitutes reasonable accommodations. The chapter ends with a summary and recommendations for educational leaders.

STUDENTS IN PUBLIC ELEMENTARY AND SECONDARY SCHOOLS

Prohibition Against Discrimination

Section 504 and the ADA are antidiscrimination statutes that prohibit school boards, educators, and others from offering unequal opportunities to otherwise qualified individuals with disabilities. Although Section 504 is tied in to the receipt of federal funds, in contrast to the IDEA and NCLB, neither Section 504 nor the ADA provides funds for school systems to use in their efforts to provide equal access to their programs.

In seeking redress for violations of either Section 504 or the ADA, students do not need to show that acts of discrimination were intentional. In a case illustrating this principle, the federal trial court in Arizona held that a school board's failure to correct a situation that resulted in a denial of access revealed that an impermissible disparate impact was sufficient to allow the plaintiff to present a discrimination claim under Section 504 (*Begay v. Hodel,* 1990). The court decided that the board violated the student's rights when officials failed to correct architectural barriers in her neighborhood high school, which, in turn, forced her to transfer to a school several miles away. This resulted in the student's having to commute over poor roads, which aggravated her condition and forced her to withdraw from school. Although school officials may not have intended to discriminate against the student with disabilities, the court concluded that their failure to take corrective action resulted in a discriminatory effect.

> In seeking redress for violations of either Section 504 or the ADA, students do not need to show that acts of discrimination were intentional.

As noted by the Second Circuit in a case from Vermont, Section 504 does not require that all individuals with disabilities receive identical benefits (*P. C. v. McLaughlin,* 1990). The court, acknowledging that courts must allow for professional judgment, stated that in order to substantiate a discrimination claim under Section 504, the plaintiff had to have demonstrated that more suitable arrangements were available but were not offered. The court maintained that the record did not substantiate a discrimination claim, because the student failed to offer proof indicating that more suitable arrangements were available than those he was offered.

School officials cannot discriminate against students with disabilities on the basis of the means by which they address their impairments. A federal trial court in California was convinced that as long as the means by which a student dealt with her circumstances were reasonable, school officials could not discriminate against her in light of how she chose to address her situation (*Sullivan v. Vallejo City Unified School District*, 1990). The court thus reasoned that educational officials violated Section 504 by refusing to allow the student to bring a service dog to school. The court added that excluding the service dog effectively prevented the student from dealing with her disability in school in the same manner that she addressed it elsewhere. Even so, that does not mean that students with disabilities can always dictate precisely how their needs will be met. For example, the federal trial court in Nebraska was of the opinion that the ADA does not provide parents with additional clout regarding the choice of methodology for instructing their children with hearing impairments in disputes over the type of signing that students should receive (*Petersen v. Hastings Public Schools*, 1993). The court insisted that since the methodology selected by school officials to instruct students with hearing impairments was no less effective than the one preferred by their parents, it met the ADA's requirements.

In a high-profile case, the federal trial court in New Jersey issued an injunction preventing a school board from retroactively changing its policies regarding the naming of a valedictorian who had a physical disability that caused substantial physical fatigue (*Hornstine v. Township of Moorestown*, 2003). The student attended school for only a portion of the day while receiving the remainder of her instruction at home. In her senior year the student received the highest weighted grade point average in her class. Rather than name her the class valedictorian, the superintendent initiated an effort to change school board policy to allow for multiple valedictorians and salutatorians. In blocking this action, the court found more than sufficient evidence that the proposed action was intended to have a particular exclusionary effect on the plaintiff because of her status as a student with disabilities.

Two noneducation cases demonstrate that school boards must not discriminate in the provision of services to students with disabilities or even among students with different kinds of disabilities. In the first, a federal trial court in Florida determined that the elimination of all recreation programs for individuals with disabilities violated the ADA in view of the fact that similar programs were still being offered to those who did not have disabilities (*Concerned Parents to Save Dreher Park Center v. City of West Palm Beach*, 1994). City officials eliminated the programs due to fiscal constraints, but the court insisted that any benefits provided to persons who did not have disabilities had to be made available on an equal basis to those with disabilities. Consequently, the court asserted that because city officials chose to provide recreation services to people who were not disabled, the ADA required them to provide equal opportunities for persons with disabilities. In the second case, a federal trial court in Pennsylvania indicated that even though a public entity was not prohibited from providing benefits, services, or advantages to individuals with disabilities or to a particular class of individuals with disabilities beyond those required by the ADA, it could not discriminate in the provision of affirmative services (*Easley v. Snider*, 1993). The court emphasized that offering services to persons with physical disabilities while not providing them to individuals with physical and mental disabilities constituted discrimination, because there was no rational reason for excluding the individuals who had mental disabilities (in addition to their physical disabilities) from the program's benefits.

On the other hand, another federal trial court in Pennsylvania ruled that a school board did not violate Section 504 when it discontinued the provision of video teleconferencing equipment to a student who was frequently absent due to illness (*Eric H. ex rel. John H. v. Methacton School District*, 2003). The teleconferencing equipment allowed the student to participate in classroom activities even when he was absent. Officials discontinued the teleconferencing, because it presented problems insofar as it was disruptive to other students and the class as a whole. The court agreed that since the student received an appropriate education under the IDEA even without the use of this equipment, he was not denied benefits to which peers had been accorded. Further, the court recognized that the board's action in discontinuing the use of the equipment was not made solely on the basis of the student's disability. The court acknowledged that the fact that the means to address the student's disabilities had a negative effect on other students was an indication that they were not reasonable.

Generally speaking, when school boards have met the requirements of the IDEA for students, courts find that the boards have not discriminated against the students under Section 504 or the ADA. In such a case, the Sixth Circuit affirmed that a school board in Kentucky did not violate Section 504 in failing to provide an extended school year program after a hearing officer thought that the IDEA did not require it to offer such a program (*Cordrey v. Euckert*, 1990). Other courts have agreed that even if school board officials fail to meet the requirements of the IDEA, students seeking redress under Section 504 or the ADA must show that such boards acted in bad faith or with gross misjudgment (*Smith v. Special School District No. 1*, 1999; *Walker v. District of Columbia*, 2001; *Wenger v. Canastota Central School District*, 1997, 1998). The failure of school officials to provide a free appropriate public education, an incorrect evaluation, or a faulty accommodation plan alone would be insufficient to demonstrate discrimination under Section 504 or the ADA (*Breen v. Charles R-IV School District*, 1997). Conversely, officials' egregious failure to implement students' individualized education programs (IEPs), revise existing IEPs when doing so is clearly warranted, or failing to implement a hearing officer's order are actionable under Section 504 and the ADA (*R. B. ex rel. L. B. v. Board of Education of the City of New York*, 2000).

Definition of Disability

In order to qualify for services under Section 504 or the ADA, students must first demonstrate that they have disabilities as defined by those statutes. This means that students must show that they have impairments that adversely affect major life activities (29 U.S.C. § 706(7)(B); 42 U.S.C. § 12102(2)). Not surprisingly, courts generally consider learning to be a major life activity, because it is explicitly covered in the regulations.

Students who have contagious diseases, such as AIDS, are deemed to have disabilities under Section 504 and the ADA, because they have physical impairments that substantially interfere with life activities (*Doe v. Dolton Elementary School District No. 148*, 1988). An early case from California dealt with the rights of a kindergarten student with AIDS who apparently bit classmates. Insofar as the student's doctor certified that there was no medical reason why he could not attend class, a federal trial court ordered educational officials to admit him to school (*Thomas v. Atascadero Unified School District*, 1987). Similarly, the Eighth Circuit was of the view that a student carrier of the hepatitis B virus was an individual with disabilities under the meaning of Section 504 (*Kohl v. Woodhaven Learning Center*, 1989). Still, students' health problems must substantially limit a major life activity such as learning in order for children to be eligible to receive services under Section 504 or the ADA (*Costello v. Mitchell Public School District 79*, 2001).

> Not surprisingly, courts generally consider learning to be a major life activity.

Students with learning disabilities or other impairments that interfere with learning are considered to be disabled under Section 504 and the ADA (*I. D. v. Westmoreland School District*, 1992). Students with learning impairments are usually covered under the IDEA and thus receive services under that statute. As indicated above, compliance with the IDEA generally translates to compliance under Section 504 and the ADA. Yet, since the IDEA does not address all nonacademic situations, Section 504 and the ADA frequently become operative when students seek to participate in extracurricular activities. In such circumstances, courts have required athletic associations to waive usual eligibility rules when students do not meet the usual participation requirements due to disabilities (Osborne & Battaglino, 1996). In an illustrative case, the high court of West Virginia ordered school officials to provide a sign-language interpreter so that a student who was hearing impaired could understand the directions of her coach and be better able to participate in athletics on an equal par with her teammates (*State of West Virginia ex rel. Lambert v. West Virginia State Board of Education*, 1994).

In 1999 the U.S. Supreme Court decided a trio of noneducation cases under the ADA that collectively stand for the proposition that mitigating, or corrective, measures may be considered when school officials determine whether a student has a disability. Even though these cases were decided in noneducation employment contexts, they have implications regarding whether students are disabled. By the same token, although this litigation involved only the ADA, due to the similarity of the statutes, the opinions in those cases also have implications for the interpretation of Section 504.

In *Sutton v. United Airlines* (*Sutton,* 1999), the Supreme Court found that if an individual is taking measures to correct for or mitigate an impairment, the effects of those actions must be considered when evaluating whether the person is substantially limited in a major life activity. Essentially, the Court differentiated between an individual currently being substantially limited, as opposed to being potentially or hypothetically substantially limited, when attempting to demonstrate the existence of a disability. Put another way, the Court pointed out that an individual whose physical or mental impairment is corrected through medication or other measures does not have an impairment that presently limits a major life activity. Under these circumstances, such a person would not meet the ADA's definition of an individual with a disability and would not be entitled to accommodations.

The Supreme Court decided the second case, *Murphy v. United Parcel Service* (1999), by referencing its previous order in *Sutton,* noting that considering whether an individual's impairment substantially limits one or more major life activities is made in view of the mitigating measures that an individual uses. In the third case, *Albertson's, Inc. v. Kirkingburg* (1999), the Court added that it does not make any difference whether corrective measures are undertaken with artificial aids, such as medication or devices, or measures taken with the body's own systems, such as learning to adapt to or compensate for impairments.

In these three cases the Supreme Court emphasized that a consideration of whether a person has a disability under the ADA must be an individual inquiry. In a later case, *Toyota Motor Manufacturing v. Williams* (2002), the Court specified that an impairment must prevent or severely restrict an individual from engaging in activities that are of central importance to most people's daily lives. Further, the Court emphasized that the impact of an impairment must be permanent or long term.

Taken together, these decisions indicate that elementary or secondary students who have impairments that can be easily corrected would not qualify as students with disabilities under either the ADA or Section 504. For example, as in *Sutton,* a student with poor vision that can be fully mitigated with corrective lenses would not have a disability. Nevertheless, it is important to recognize that many corrective devices improve functioning for individuals but may not fully mitigate the effects of their impairments. For this reason, educational officials must conduct individualized assessments when considering whether impairments, even when partially corrected, limit major life activities. In elementary or secondary schools, the inquiry as to whether students have disabilities needs to consider, among other things, whether the students' impairments affect the major life activity of learning.

An issue that has not been addressed is whether students, or other individuals, who choose not to use available mitigating measures or devices would qualify as individuals with disabilities under Section 504 and the ADA. For example, many students are given medication for attention deficit hyperactivity disorder, but, for various reasons, some parents choose not to have their children take the psychotropic medications that are usually prescribed. In such instances, when impairments can be fully mitigated through use of medications, it is unclear whether students would qualify as disabled under Section 504 and the ADA if their parents are unwilling to have them take the medications. It is also important to keep in mind that the IDEA prohibits states, and school systems, from requiring children to take medications as a condition of attending school, being evaluated, or receiving services (20 U.S.C. § 1412(a)(25)). Even so, it remains to be seen whether courts will interpret Section 504 and the ADA as not allowing school personnel to consider whether parents subject their children to corrective measures in order to mitigate impairments in evaluating their eligibility for or the provision of services.

Otherwise Qualified Students With Disabilities

Once students can demonstrate that they have impairments that affect a major life activity, they must then demonstrate that they are otherwise qualified to participate in educational programs. The U.S. Supreme Court, in *Southeastern Community College v. Davis* (*Davis*, 1979), its first case interpreting the provisions of Section 504, provided a definition of "otherwise qualified." The Court explained that in order to be considered otherwise qualified, students with disabilities must be able to participate in programs or activities in spite of their impairments as long as they can do so with reasonable accommodations. Even though the student in *Davis* was in a postsecondary program, its implications are the same for elementary and secondary school students.

Students with disabilities must meet all of the usual qualifications for participation in the school's programs. The student who filed suit in *Davis* challenged her being denied admission to a nursing program because she was hearing impaired and relied on lip reading to understand speech. In upholding the actions of the program officials who denied the student's application due to safety considerations, the Court interpreted Section 504 as not requiring educational institutions to disregard the disabilities of applicants or to make substantial modifications to their programs to allow participation. The Court acknowledged that legitimate physical qualifications could be essential to participation in programs.

A federal trial court in Kentucky applied the reasoning from *Davis* in deciding that a student with multiple disabilities who was denied admission to the state's school for the blind was not otherwise qualified. According to the court, because the student did not meet the school's admission criteria—that applicants demonstrate ability for academic and vocational learning, self-care, and independent functioning—she was not qualified for admission (*Eva N. v. Brock*, 1990). While the court held that officials did not have to admit the student to its school for the blind, it advised them that the IDEA still obligated them to provide her with a free appropriate public education. On the other hand, a federal trial court in Tennessee declared that a student, who suffered from an autoimmune disease of the blood system that could have resulted in life-threatening hemorrhaging, was otherwise qualified to attend a private school, because she had the necessary academic qualifications (*Thomas v. Davidson Academy*, 1994). The court asserted that expelling the student, following an incident where she became hysterical after cutting herself with a knife, violated both Section 504 and the ADA, because such behavior could have been dealt with leniently in light of her situation.

> To be considered otherwise qualified, students with disabilities must be able to participate in programs or activities in spite of their impairments as long as they can do so with reasonable accommodations.

In a disagreement over sports participation, the Seventh Circuit confirmed that a coach in Indiana who refused to select a student for the high school's basketball team did not violate his rights under Section 504 (*Doe v. Eagle-Union Community School Corporation*, 2001a). The court was convinced that even though the student had a Section 504 alternative learning plan, the coach did not select him for the team because he lacked the requisite skills. The court thus affirmed that the student was not otherwise qualified for participation. The Supreme Court refused to hear a further appeal in the case (*Doe v. Eagle-Union Community School Corporation*, 2001b).

Reasonable Accommodations

Section 504 and the ADA do not always require school boards, and the officials charged with carrying out their dictates, to disregard completely the disabilities of those who wish to participate in their programs and activities. Still, educational officials must allow individuals to participate when doing so would require them only to make reasonable accommodations. This means that educators are not required to make substantial modifications or fundamental alterations of programs and activities (*Southeastern Community College v. Davis*, 1979). The requirement to provide reasonable accommodations to allow individuals with disabilities to participate does not carry with it the obligation for school boards to lower their standards. Reasonable accommodations do require adaptations to allow access, but they do not direct school officials to eliminate essential prerequisites to participation or to make substantial alterations to the nature of their programs.

> The requirement to provide reasonable accommodations to allow individuals with disabilities to participate does not carry with it an obligation for school boards to lower their standards.

Appropriate Education

Otherwise qualified students are entitled to an appropriate public education, regardless of the nature or severity of their disabilities. In order to ensure that students receive an appropriate education, Section 504's regulations include due process procedures for evaluation and placement similar to those of the IDEA (34 C.F.R. § 104.36).

When school officials offer accommodations for students, they must make aid, benefits, and/or services available that are comparable to those existing for children who do not have disabilities. More specifically, otherwise qualified students must receive comparable materials, teacher quality, length of school term, and daily hours of instruction. In addition, programs for otherwise qualified students should not be separate from those available to students who do not have disabilities, unless such segregation is necessary for these programs to be effective. While school officials are not prohibited from offering separate programs for students who have impairments, these children cannot be required to attend such classes, unless they cannot be served adequately in inclusive settings (34 C.F.R. § 104.4(b)(3)). If programs are offered separately, facilities must, of course, be comparable (34 C.F.R. § 104.34(c); *Hendricks v. Gilhool*, 1989). Further, nothing in the statutes or their regulations prohibits school boards from centralizing services for students with disabilities (*Barnett v. Fairfax County School Board*, 1989, 1991). However, students cannot be required to attend centralized programs if the locations of such programs present obstacles to the students' participation (*Begay v. Hodel*, 1990).

Over the past two decades, parents have increasingly filed suits under the IDEA seeking programs in fully inclusive settings for their children with severe disabilities. In addition to the IDEA, courts have turned to Section 504 for guidance in evaluating whether placements in inclusionary settings are legally required. In one such case, the federal trial court in New Jersey, in a judgment that the Third Circuit affirmed, was convinced that excluding a student from the regular education classroom without first investigating and providing reasonable accommodations violated Section 504 (*Oberti v. Board of Education of the Borough of Clementon School District*, 1992, 1993). The court remarked that a segregated special education placement can be the program of choice only when it is necessary for a child to receive educational benefit.

Reasonable accommodations may involve minor adjustments for students. Courts have allowed such accommodations as providing a hearing interpreter for a student (*Barnes v. Converse College*, 1977), permitting a child to be accompanied by a service dog (*Sullivan v. Vallejo City Unified School District*, 1990), modifying a behavior policy to accommodate a student who was disruptive (*Thomas v. Davidson Academy*, 1994), and using nonverbal signals to make a student aware of inappropriate sensory stimulations and giving her preferred seating in the school lunchroom to minimize environmental influences that might have disrupted her ability to concentrate on the task at hand (*Molly L. ex rel. B. L. v. Lower Merion School District*, 2002).

Pursuant to Section 504 and the ADA, school personnel do not have to grant all requests for accommodations. For example, a federal trial court in Missouri insisted that school officials did not have to maintain a "scent-free" environment for a child with severe asthma, because she was not otherwise qualified to participate in its educational program (*Hunt v. St. Peter School*, 1997). The court added that the school's voluntary scent-free policy met Section 504's "minor adjustment" standard. Another federal trial court, this one in Pennsylvania, decided that school officials did not violate the Section 504 rights of a student who was classified as other health impaired when they discontinued video teleconferencing equipment that allowed him to participate in classroom activities when he was absent (*Eric H. ex rel. John H. v. Methacton School District*, 2003). The court, ruling that school officials did not violate Section 504 because the student was not denied benefits that would have been provided to children who were not disabled, agreed with the school board's assessment that the presence of the equipment in the classroom was disruptive to other students in the class. A federal trial court in New York upheld the actions of school officials who refused to allow a student with hearing impairments to bring his service dog to school in determining that they had already adequately accommodated his disabilities (*Cave v. East Meadow Union Free School District*, 2007). The court was apparently swayed by evidence that the dog could pose a problem for other students and teachers who suffered from allergies. Taken together, these cases illustrate the fact that any offered accommodations must take into consideration the effect they will have on others in the program. If requested accommodations will have a negative effect on others who participate in programs, then they may not be reasonable.

On the other hand, the Second Circuit ruled that school officials in New York who refused to provide reasonable accommodations to a student who was unable to attend school due to a chronic illness presented actionable claims under both Section 504 and the ADA (*Weixel v. Board of Education of the City of New York,* 2002). The court thought that accommodations, such as not requiring the student to climb stairs if she felt too sick and allowing her to lie down on a couch if she needed to rest, were reasonable. In another case, school officials forced a student with asthma to perform physical exercise as a punishment, thereby triggering an attack of his illness. Not surprisingly, a federal trial court in Tennessee reasoned that school personnel violated the student's rights under the ADA (*Moss v. Shelby County,* 2005). The court was convinced that educators should have modified their standard punishment to accommodate the student's asthma. As this latter case reveals, it is imperative for school officials to make sure that all employees are well aware of disabled students' conditions and are provided with proper training to make sure that such situations do not have tragic consequences.

Academic modifications might include giving children more time to take examinations or finish assignments, using peer tutors, distributing outlines in advance, employing specialized curricular materials, or permitting students to use laptop computers to take examinations. When modifying facilities, school boards do not have to make every classroom or area of school buildings accessible. Generally, it is acceptable to bring services to children; an example might be offering keyboards for musical instruction in accessible classrooms, rather than revamping entire music rooms for disabled students who wish to take piano lessons.

In an early case from Texas, the Supreme Court required a school board to provide basic school health services to a student with physical impairments. The services, which allowed the student to be present in a classroom, were considered to be a reasonable accommodation (*Tatro v. State of Texas,* 1980, 1981, 1983, 1984). The student needed to be catheterized approximately every four hours, and this service could be easily provided by a school nurse, health aide, or other trained layperson. The Court ruled that when school officials refused to provide such a service, they violated the student's Section 504 rights.

Athletics

Disputes often arise over whether school boards and athletic associations can be required to waive nonessential eligibility requirements for participation in sports or other extracurricular activities. The results are mixed and are often dependent on the unique facts of each situation.

On the one hand, at least two courts ordered athletic associations to waive age limitation requirements to allow students who repeated grades due to their learning disabilities to participate in sports (*Hoot v. Milan Area Schools*, 1994; *University Interscholastic League v. Buchanan*, 1993). These courts agreed that where the association allowed waivers of other rules, a waiver of the one prohibiting students over the age of 19 from participating in sports was a reasonable accommodation. In a related situation, the Sixth Circuit maintained that in preventing a transfer student from participating in sports when he changed schools only because of his need to receive special education services, officials violated his rights under Section 504 (*Crocker v. Tennessee Secondary School Athletic Association*, 1990).

On the other hand, in an admittedly different factual context, the Sixth Circuit later decided that a high school athletic association's eight-semester eligibility rule did not violate either Section 504 or the ADA, since a student's claim that it violated his rights was without merit (*McPherson v. Michigan High School Athletic Association*, 1997). Earlier, the Eighth Circuit indicated that since a student who challenged an athletic association's age restrictions was not otherwise qualified under either the ADA or Section 504 because he exceeded the age limit, he was not entitled to relief (*Pottgen v. Missouri State High School Activities Association*, 1994).

A federal trial court in Illinois, in another case involving sports, rejected the claims of a student-athlete who was suspended from his football and lacrosse teams for disciplinary infractions (*Long v. Board of Education, District 128*, 2001). The court pointed out that waiving the athletic code of conduct would have been an unreasonable accommodation under Section 504 and the ADA, because it would have sent the message to others that student-athletes could thwart the enforcement of team rules by threatening legal actions. This, in the court's opinion, would have made it difficult for school officials to maintain effective control over their athletic programs.

Testing Accommodations

Most jurisdictions have implemented requirements that students pass comprehensive state-administered tests to graduate with standard high school diplomas. This prerequisite has become more prevalent following the passage of the No Child Left Behind Act. In addition, some public schools may require students, including those with disabilities, to take admissions examinations and/or be interviewed prior to being accepted and/or placed. These procedures may be initiated to evaluate whether applicants are otherwise qualified. Under Section 504 and the ADA, school boards may be required to modify test-taking situations to allow students with disabilities to complete their examinations on an equal footing with their peers. The Section 504 regulations address this situation, covering four areas: preplacement evaluation, evaluation, placement, and reevaluation (34 C.F.R. § 104.35).

With respect to preplacement evaluations, the regulations oblige school officials to evaluate all children who, because of their impairments, need or are believed to need special education or related services. This assessment is to be completed before school officials take any action with respect to the children's initial placements in regular or special education as well as before any subsequent significant changes in placement occur.

Section 504's evaluation provisions require school officials to follow procedures similar to those under the IDEA. In particular, educators must validate tests and other evaluation materials for the specific purposes for which they are used, and the tests must be administered by trained personnel in conformance with the instructions provided by their producer. Further, materials must be tailored to assess specific areas of educational need and cannot be designed to provide a single general intelligence quotient. Test materials must be chosen and administered in a manner that best ensures that when they are administered to students with impaired sensory, manual, or speaking skills, the results accurately reflect their aptitude or achievement level (or whatever other factor the test purports to measure) rather than their impaired sensory, manual, or speaking skills, except where those skills are the factors that the tests purport to measure. When school officials apply placement procedures to students covered under Section 504, the officials' interpretations of data must consider information from a variety of sources, including results of aptitude and achievement tests, teacher recommendations, and each student's physical condition, social and cultural background, and adaptive behaviors that have been documented and carefully considered. Not only must such decisions be made by groups of persons, including individuals who are knowledgeable, but children must also be periodically reevaluated in a manner consistent with the requirements of the IDEA.

Schools relying on examinations or interviews may be required to provide reasonable accommodations to applicants with disabilities. Although school officials are not required to alter the content of examinations or interviews, they may have to make accommodations in how tests are administered or interviews are conducted. Accordingly, school authorities would not be required to make examinations easier so that students who simply lacked the requisite knowledge could pass, but they would have to alter the situations under which examinations are administered, or interviews are conducted, so that students with disabilities who have the requisite knowledge and skills to pass or express themselves fully could do so in spite of their circumstances.

The accommodations that educators provide for examinations may be as simple as procuring the services of readers or providing Braille versions of examinations for applicants who are visually impaired, extending time requirements for students who have learning disabilities, or providing distraction-free settings for students with attention deficit hyperactivity disorder. Students with physical disabilities may need to be provided with special seating arrangements, scribes to record answers to questions, or computers to record answers on examinations. In the same way, whether as part of examinations or admissions interviews, students who are hearing impaired might require the services of sign-language interpreters to communicate directions that are normally given orally. At the same time, school officials may be obligated to make computers available to children who have difficulty with traditional paper-and-pencil tests.

In order to receive accommodations, students must show that the accommodations are required because they have disabilities (*Argen v. New York State Board of Law Examiners,* 1994) and that the accommodations are necessary due to the students' impairments. For instance, one purpose of providing extra time on examinations is to allow students with learning disabilities who might have difficulty processing information sufficient opportunity to show that they are capable of answering the questions.

A significant difference between the IDEA, which requires school officials to identify, assess, and serve students with disabilities, and Section 504 or the ADA is that students and/or their parents are responsible under the latter statutes for making school officials aware of the fact that they need accommodations. Thus, those responsible for administering examinations may require proof that students have impairments in need of accommodation in order to demonstrate knowledge and skills on examinations. Students, through their parents, should also suggest which accommodations would be most appropriate. When considering whether students are entitled to accommodations, school officials must make individualized inquiries. Educators would likely violate Section 504 and the ADA if they refused to make testing accommodations or made modifications only for students with specified impairments.

At the same time, it is well-settled that school boards are not required to alter the content of the tests themselves (*Brookhart v. Illinois State Board of Education,* 1983). The courts generally agree that altering the content of tests to accommodate the inability of individuals to learn amounts to a substantial modification. Then again, modifying the manner in which tests are administered to accommodate student disabilities would, in most circumstances, be considered to be reasonable. In this way, allowing students who are visually impaired to take Braille versions of tests is a reasonable accommodation, but changing the content of examinations to make them easier would probably not be required. One exception might involve modifying items on a test that are based on an experience that the student might not have because of the disability. By way of illustration, a test item that asks students to describe what a cell looks like under a microscope would be unfair on a test given to an individual who was never able to look through a microscope due to being blind.

Most of the disputes over testing accommodations have been litigated in the context of postsecondary institutions and are discussed in a later section on students in higher education. Even so, much of the litigation applies to situations in elementary and secondary schools. These cases help to demonstrate the point that accommodations in how tests are administered are reasonable, but alterations to their contents are not. In one such case, a federal trial court in New York ordered additional accommodations for a visually impaired law school graduate who was sitting for the bar examination. The Board of Bar Examiners granted some, but not all, of the graduate's requested accommodations. Yet, the court ordered additional accommodations that her doctor testified were necessary, on the ground that the purpose of the ADA was to guarantee that those with disabilities are not disadvantaged but are put on an equal footing with others (*D'Amico v. New York State Board of Law Examiners*, 1993). Another case from New York involving a law school graduate demonstrated that applicants are not entitled to accommodations just because they may have failed examinations in the past without such adjustments (*Pazer v. New York State Board of Law Examiners*, 1994). The court commented that requested accommodations were not necessary for a student who claimed to have a learning disability where the testimony of an acknowledged expert on dyslexia proved to be credible and persuasive in establishing that he did not have such a condition.

Undue Burden

Accommodations that are unduly costly, create an excessive monitoring burden, or expose other individuals to excessive risk are not required. For example, the Eighth Circuit stipulated that inoculating staff members against the hepatitis B virus so that a carrier of that disease could attend a learning center program went beyond the requirements of Section 504

(*Kohl v. Woodhaven Learning Center,* 1989). Similarly, a federal trial court in Kentucky ruled that a school for the blind could not be required to hire additional staff or modify its mission by accepting a student who did not meet its minimum admissions qualifications (*Eva N. v. Brock,* 1990).

One of the main differences between the IDEA and Section 504 or the ADA is that in order to be eligible under the IDEA, students must require special education. Under this principle, while students with disabilities who do not require special education services but need accommodations in order to access educational services may not be covered by the IDEA but may be protected under Section 504 and the ADA. In such a situation, the Second Circuit, in a dispute from Vermont, affirmed that Section 504 does not require a school board to provide students with disabilities with potential-maximizing educational services (*J. D. v. Pawlett School District,* 2000). Rather, the court explained that Section 504 only requires school officials to make reasonable accommodations that give qualified students the same access to the benefits of a public education as their peers who are not disabled.

Section 504/ADA Service Plans

Otherwise qualified students under Section 504 or the ADA are entitled to reasonable accommodations so that they may access school facilities and programs. As indicated above, many accommodations involve alterations to physical plants, such as building wheelchair ramps or removing architectural barriers, so that students may physically enter and get around school buildings (*Begay v. Hodel,* 1990). Students may also address their disabilities in school environments as they do elsewhere such as by bringing service dogs into classrooms (*Sullivan v. Vallejo City Unified School District,* 1990). Section 504 and the ADA do not mandate that school officials provide accommodations that go beyond what would be considered to be reasonable. In this respect, accommodations that are excessively expensive, that expose the school's staff or other students to excessive risk, or that require school officials to make substantial modifications to the missions or purposes of programs are not required (*Eva N. v. Brock,* 1990; *Kohl v. Woodhaven Learning Center,* 1989).

It is clear that Section 504, the ADA, and their regulations, unlike the IEP provisions in the IDEA, do not call for the creation of written agreements with regard to student accommodations or specify the content of such documents. Nevertheless, school officials in many districts wisely meet with parents to formalize the accommodations and services that they will provide to eligible students and commit their agreements to writing. These written agreements are generally referred to as service plans, even though the term is found nowhere in Section 504, the ADA, or their regulations. Insofar as there is no requirement to put service plans into writing, there are no stipulations as to the contents of service plans. In practical terms, school officials should include the following components in each written Section 504 or ADA service plan (Russo & Osborne, 2007):

Demographic Data: Student's name, date of birth, school identification number, school, grade, teacher, parents' names, address, telephone numbers, and the like.

Team Members: A listing of all team members who contributed to the development of the service plan and their respective positions and roles.

Impairment: A description of the student's impairment and its severity along with an explanation of how it impedes the child's educational progress.

Accommodations and Services: A detailed description of the accommodations and services to be offered under the plan, including the frequency and location of services and by whom they will be provided.

Team members should also reference or attach the evaluative reports or assessments that helped to determine the nature of a student's impairment and the need for accommodations and services. Figure 3.1 shows a form that can be used for such a plan.

STUDENTS IN NONPUBLIC SCHOOLS

To the extent that Section 504 is not predicated on the direct receipt of federal assistance, it applies to nonpublic schools (34 C.F.R. § 104.39), because the interpretation of financial aid has been broad (*Bob Jones University v. United States*, 1983; *Hunt v. St. Peter School*, 1997). To this end, Section 504 prohibits discrimination in nonpublic schools by requiring educators to make individualized modifications for otherwise qualified students with disabilities. This means that all schools, including those that are nonpublic, assuming that they have admitted children pursuant to Section 504, must provide aid, benefits, and/or services that are comparable to those available to students who are not disabled. Under these provisions, children with disabilities must receive comparable materials, teacher quality, length of school term, and daily hours of instruction. In addition, the ADA does apply to nonpublic schools except for those that are affiliated with religious entities (*Doe v. Abington Friends School*, 2007; *White v. Denver Seminary*, 2001).

Figure 3.1   Sample Section 504/ADA Service Plan

Student's Name: _____ Date of Birth: _____ ID Number: _____

School: _____ Teacher: _____ Grade: _____

Parents: _____

Address: _____ Telephone Number: _____

Team Members: Position/ Role:

_____   _____

_____   _____

_____   _____

_____   _____

_____   _____

_____   _____

Impairment: (Please provide a complete description of the student's impairment, including information about its severity along with a description about how it affects the student.)

Accommodations: (Please provide a detailed description of the accommodations and/or services that will be provided to the student, including information about the frequency and location of services and by whom they will be provided.)

_____   _____
School Official's Signature   Parent's Signature

Programs for students with disabilities in nonpublic schools should not be separate from those available to peers who are not disabled, unless such segregation is necessary for the programs to be effective. While schools are not prohibited from offering separate programs for students with disabilities, these children cannot be required to attend such classes unless they cannot be served adequately in a regular classroom setting (34 C.F.R. § 104.4(b)(3)). If such programs are offered separately, facilities must, of course, be comparable (34 C.F.R. § 104.34(c)). If schools offer special programs for students with disabilities, they may not charge more for such services "except to the extent that any additional charge is justified by a substantial increase in cost" (34 C.F.R. § 104.39(b)).

> Programs for students with disabilities in nonpublic schools should not be separate from those available to peers who are not disabled, unless such segregation is necessary for the program to be effective.

Once identified, qualified students with disabilities are entitled to an appropriate public education, regardless of the nature or severity of their disabilities. In order to guarantee that an appropriate education is made available, Section 504's regulations include due process requirements for evaluation and placement similar to those under the IDEA (34 C.F.R. § 104.36).

Finally, Section 504, which is enforced by the Office of Civil Rights, requires each recipient of federal financial aid to file an assurance of compliance; provide notice to students and their parents that their programs are nondiscriminatory; engage in remedial actions where violations are proven; take voluntary steps to overcome the effects of conditions that resulted in limiting the participation of students with disabilities in their programs; conduct a self-evaluation; designate a staff member, typically at the central office level, as compliance coordinator; and adopt grievance procedures (34 C.F.R. § 104.5).

Admissions Examinations/Standards

Many nonpublic schools, including those that consider admitting students with disabilities, require applicants to take admissions examinations and/or be interviewed prior to acceptance or placement in order to determine whether they are otherwise qualified. Not surprisingly, since Section 504 specifically addresses evaluation and placement procedures (34 C.F.R. § 104.35), schools are not obligated to accept students who are not otherwise qualified. In one such case, the Second Circuit ruled that officials at a private high school in Vermont did not have to enroll a student who was unable to read at a fifth grade level. Insofar as the student was not otherwise qualified for a high school program, the court concluded that the officials were under no obligation to lower the school's requirements and admit the student (*St. Johnsbury Academy v. D. H.*, 2001).

Under Section 504 and the ADA, nonpublic schools that rely on examinations and/or interviews may be required to provide reasonable accommodations to applicants with disabilities. As with public schools, while officials are not required to alter the content of examinations or interviews, they may be required to make accommodations in how a test is administered or an interview is conducted. In other words, school officials would not be required to make an examination easier so that students who simply lacked the requisite knowledge could pass (*Tips v. Regents of Texas Tech University*, 1996), but they may have to alter the conditions under which examinations are administered, or interviews are conducted, so that students with disabilities with the requisite knowledge and skills to pass or express themselves fully can do so in spite of their disabilities.

> Under Section 504 and the ADA, schools that rely on examinations or interviews may be required to provide reasonable accommodations to applicants who have disabilities.

Accommodations for examinations may be as simple as providing a quiet room without distractions, essentially a private room away from others, for students who suffer from attention deficit hyperactivity disorder or procuring the services of readers or Braille versions of examinations for applicants who are blind. Further, officials may have to provide students with physical disabilities with special seating arrangements, scribes to record answers to questions, or computers to record answers on examinations. Similarly, whether for examinations or admissions interviews, students who are hearing impaired might be entitled to the services of sign-language interpreters to communicate directions that are normally given orally. At the same time, school officials may be required to provide students with learning disabilities with extra time in which to complete examinations, or they may need to make computers available to children who may be more comfortable with technology than with traditional paper-and-pencil tests.

Prior to receiving extra time for examinations, students, usually through their parents, must prove that they have learning disabilities (*Argen v. New York State Board of Law Examiners, 1994)*, and that the extra time is necessary due to their learning disabilities (*Gonzalez v. National Board of Medical Examiners*, 1999; *Price v. National Board of Medical Examiners*, 1997). Again, the purpose of providing the extra time would be to allow students who might have difficulty processing information sufficient opportunity to show that they are capable of answering the questions. It is the responsibility of students (and/or their parents) to make school officials aware of the fact that they are disabled and need testing accommodations. To this end, principals and other officials in nonpublic (and public, as noted) schools should require proof that students have impairments in need of accommodation in order for them to demonstrate knowledge and skills on examinations. Students, through their parents, should also suggest which accommodations would be most appropriate. In considering whether students are entitled to accommodations, school officials must make individualized inquiries. Educators would violate Section 504 if they refused to make testing accommodations or made modifications only for students with specified disabilities.

STUDENTS IN HIGHER EDUCATION

Discriminatory Practices Prohibited

In order to bring successful discrimination claims, students need to demonstrate that they suffered from adverse actions due to their disabilities. Students with disabilities have been unsuccessful where educational officials can show that they had legitimate, nondiscriminatory reasons for acting. In one such case, a federal trial court in New York could not uncover evidence of discrimination on the part of university officials who dismissed a student with cerebral palsy from its doctoral program (*Villanueva v. Columbia University*, 1990). In fact, the court pointed out that the student was dismissed from the program because of her unsatisfactory academic performance. Similarly, the Eighth Circuit dismissed the discrimination claims of a student in Minnesota who was dismissed from medical school after failing several courses. The court acknowledged that the student was not discharged solely because of his learning disabilities (*Falcone v. University of Minnesota*, 2004). More recently, the same court determined that a university was justified in barring a student with disabilities who threatened a faculty member's life (*Mershon v. St. Louis University*, 2006). The court was convinced that university officials demonstrated the existence of a legitimate nondiscriminatory reason in excluding the student. On the other hand, a federal trial court in North Carolina reasoned that officials discriminated against a student who was cut from the golf team because he missed practice to attend medical appointments that were needed because of his disability (*Costello v. University of North Carolina at Greensboro*, 2005).

As illustrated by a case from the District of Columbia, officials at institutions of higher learning are required to conduct individualized inquiries into persons' situations before making decisions. Under this analysis, the court posited that a diabetic cadet at a merchant marine academy was improperly dismissed due to his medical condition (*Lane v. Pena*, 1994).

The court ascertained that officials discharged the student solely on the basis of his disability without either attempting to provide him with reasonable accommodations or making an individualized inquiry into his situation. Conversely, a federal trial court in Georgia upheld a medical school's dismissal of a student with reading difficulties (*Ellis v. Morehouse School of Medicine*, 1996). The court recognized that officials dismissed the student due to his unsatisfactory performance, after making a number of programmatic accommodations. The court was persuaded by the testimony of the plaintiff's instructors that he did not meet the essential requirements of a medical student, because he continued to fail courses despite the fact that they made accommodations in attempting to try to help him to succeed.

> In order to bring successful discrimination claims, students need to demonstrate that they suffered from adverse actions due to their disabilities.

Disability

In order to be covered under Section 504 and the ADA, students must first prove that they have disabilities as defined by these statutes. In many cases, the determination of whether students have covered disabilities is an individualized inquiry that may well depend on the facts of a particular situation. For example, a federal trial court in Massachusetts, noting that pregnancy is not covered by Section 504 or the ADA, acknowledged that pregnancy-related conditions that had disabling consequences could be covered (*Darian v. University of Massachusetts Boston*, 1997). On the other hand, the Tenth Circuit affirmed that an anxiety disorder that was limited to certain subjects did not constitute a disability under Section 504 or the ADA (*McGuiness v. University of New Mexico School of Medicine, 1998*). In this case, the student unsuccessfully claimed to have experienced anxiety in chemistry and mathematics courses.

Three cases in which students requested testing accommodations illustrate the point that inquiries into whether plaintiffs have disabilities under Section 504 and the ADA must be individualized and fact-specific. Moreover, these cases reveal that impairments may be considered disabilities for one person but not for another. Insofar as a great deal depends on the degree to which impairments affect individuals' abilities to participate in major life activities, this can vary from one individual to another and from one activity to another.

> The determination of whether students have covered disabilities is an individualized inquiry that may well depend on the facts of a particular situation.

A federal trial court in Michigan declared that substantially limiting impairments cannot be minor or trivial but must restrict an individual's major life activity as to the conditions, manner, or duration under which the activity can be performed in comparison to most people (*Gonzalez v. National Board of Medical Examiners*, 1999). The court determined that a student who claimed a learning deficiency did not have a disability as defined by the ADA, because his test scores were squarely in the average to superior range. Similarly, a federal trial court in Illinois ruled that a medical student with dyslexia failed to prove that his impairment would have substantially limited a major life activity without accommodations (*Biank v. National Board of Medical Examiners*, 2000). The court rejected the student's requested testing accommodations on the ground that he failed to show that his dyslexia would have significantly limited his ability to pass the examination as compared to an average person in his circumstances. Conversely, a federal trial court in Texas observed that a medical student proved that he had a disability, because he was substantially limited in the major life activities of reading and learning when compared to most people (*Rush v. National Board of Medical Examiners*, 2003).

The Ninth Circuit concluded that a medical student in California who had been diagnosed as having a disability in the way he processed verbal information did not qualify as disabled under Section 504 or the ADA (*Wong v. Regents of the University of California*, 1999). The court was of the opinion that the fact that the student had achieved a level of academic success during his first two years of medical school without any special accommodations made implausible the proposition that his impairment substantially limited his ability to learn. Similarly, a federal trial court in West Virginia upheld a decision by the National Board of Medical Examiners to deny testing accommodations for several students who had attention deficit hyperactivity disorder (*Price v. National Board of Medical Examiners*, 1997). The court observed that although each student had some learning difficulty, each had a history of significant scholastic achievement that reflected a complete absence of any substantial limitation on the ability to learn.

Ironically, prior academic success may be an indicator that a student's learning impairment does not affect the major life activity of learning rather than necessarily showing that a student has succeeded in spite of the disability. This is illustrated by two decisions handed down the same day by the federal trial court in the District of Columbia. Each decision involved a student at the same college. In the first decision the court concluded that a student who had been diagnosed as dyslexic did not have a disability as defined by the ADA, because she had enjoyed academic success throughout her life (*Singh v. George Washington University*, 2006). For similar reasons, the court in the second decision determined that a student who suffered from attention deficit disorder and a learning disability did not have a disability as defined by the ADA, because he had also enjoyed a great deal of academic success throughout his life (*Steere v. George Washington University*, 2006).

In the earlier section on students in elementary and secondary schools, three decisions by the Supreme Court were reviewed that, when taken together, indicate that mitigating or corrective measures may be considered when school officials are assessing a student's impairment (*Albertson's, Inc. v. Kirkingburg*, 1999; *Murphy v. United Parcel Service*, 1999; *Sutton v. United Air Lines*, 1999). The federal trial court in Massachusetts held that a student with a visual impairment could not claim a disability due to his eyesight because, when corrected, it did not substantially limit a major life activity (*Pacella v. Tufts University School of Dental Medicine*, 1999).

> Prior academic success may be an indicator that a student's learning impairment does not affect the major life activity of learning.

Otherwise Qualified Students With Disabilities

As noted, courts do not uphold discrimination claims if students with disabilities do not meet minimum requirements for admission or continuation in educational programs. In *Davis* the Supreme Court declared that to be considered otherwise qualified, students with disabilities must be able to participate in programs or activities in spite of their impairments as long as they can do so with reasonable accommodations. Courts have generally held that an otherwise qualified student is one who is able to meet a program's requirements in spite of the disability. For instance, the Eighth Circuit upheld the decision of officials at a university in Missouri to deny graduate school admission to a student with disabilities who never completed his application, lacked undergraduate preparation, and had a substandard academic performance (*Mershon v. St. Louis University*, 2006).

Institutions of higher education may dismiss students with disabilities for failing to meet normal academic requirements. The Fourth Circuit affirmed a university's dismissal of a pre-medical student who did not maintain a minimum grade point average in spite of having received accommodations (*Betts v. Rector and Visitors of the University of Virginia*, 2005). Similarly, the federal trial court in Massachusetts rejected a discrimination claim filed by a former student who was dismissed from a graduate program after failing two courses and receiving an unsatisfactory grade in a third (*El Kouni v. Trustees of Boston University*, 2001).

> Courts have generally held that an otherwise qualified student is one who is able to meet a program's requirements in spite of the disability.

In the sports arena, courts generally uphold actions by school officials that students with disabilities are not otherwise qualified if they are unable to meet minimum qualifications for making teams. In this respect, at least two courts supported actions of school officials that students with disabilities were not otherwise qualified due to medical conditions. In the first case, a team physician disqualified a student from playing football due to his having a congenitally narrow cervical canal (*Pahulu v. University of Kansas,* 1995). Although other doctors certified that the student could play football without any greater risk of permanent paralysis, the federal trial court in Kansas was unwilling to substitute its judgment for that of university officials. Similarly, the Seventh Circuit, stating that medical decisions are best left to team doctors and university officials, upheld a determination by university personnel in Illinois that a student with a heart problem should not play interscholastic basketball (*Knapp v. Northwestern University,* 1996). In each of these cases the courts expressed the view that participating in sports is not a major life activity.

Reasonable Accommodations

Post-secondary schools are not required to lower their admission standards or provide more than reasonable accommodations to accept students with disabilities. A federal trial court in Maine upheld a school's decision to deny transfer admission to a student who had a learning disability (*Halasz v. University of New England,* 1993). The court found that the student was not academically qualified for admission, since he did not meet the school's minimum grade point average requirements. The court noted that an educational institution is not required to lower its admission standards to accommodate students with disabilities. In another case the Supreme Court of Ohio affirmed a medical school's denial of a blind student's application to medical school on the ground that the accommodations that she sought were not reasonable. The court thought that the requested accommodations would have required fundamental alterations to the essential nature of the program and/or imposed undue financial or administrative burdens on the school (*Ohio Civil Rights Commission v. Case Western Reserve University,* 1996).

> Post-secondary schools are not required to lower their admission standards or provide any more than reasonable accommodations to accept students with disabilities.

Once admitted to schools, students with disabilities must meet the usual requirements for advancement. Even though schools may be required to provide reasonable accommodations so that students can achieve, they are not required to alter their fundamental requirements. For the most part, courts defer to school officials in evaluating whether requirements are essential to the nature of their programs (*Kaltenberger v. Ohio College of*

Podiatric Medicine, 1998). This is especially true when officials can demonstrate the existence of a relationship between their requirements and what is expected by the professions that the programs are preparing students to enter. In one such case, the Fifth Circuit affirmed a law school's refusal to advance a student to the next level because he had not attained the requisite cumulative grade point average (*McGregor v. Louisiana State University Board of Supervisors*, 1993). The court interpreted

> Even though schools may be required to provide reasonable accommodations so that a student can achieve, they are not required to alter their fundamental requirements.

Section 504 as not requiring law school officials to lower the institution's academic standards or compromise the reasonable policies of its academic program. Similarly, the Ninth Circuit affirmed that officials at a medical school who provided reasonable accommodations to a student with learning disabilities were not required to provide further accommodations that would have substantially modified the curriculum (*Zukle v. Regents of the University of California*, 1999). In yet another instance, the Second Circuit refused to order officials at a medical school in Connecticut to modify testing requirements in a manner that would have altered the nature and substance of the school's program (*Powell v. National Board of Medical Examiners*, 2004).

A case from the Eleventh Circuit illustrates the fact that accommodations provided to students with disabilities should allow them to access programs to the same degree as their peers. A student challenged a university's practice of providing accessible transportation for only four hours per day. The court ruled that providing acces-

> Accommodations provided to students with disabilities should allow them to access programs to the same degree as their peers.

sible transportation for such a limited time was not equivalent to or as effective as the transportation services offered to students without disabilities who had access to transportation twelve hours per day (*United States v. Board of Trustees for the University of Alabama*, 1990).

Much litigation has involved the denial of requests for testing accommodations for students with disabilities. As is the case with students in elementary and secondary schools, institutions of higher education must provide accommodations in how tests are administered but are not required to modify the contents of the tests themselves. The purpose of testing accommodations is to allow students to be tested effectively on their knowledge and not their disabilities (*Rush v. National Board of Medical Examiners*, 2003). In an earlier case, the First Circuit upheld the decision of officials at a medical school in Massachusetts to require a student to take written multiple choice exams (*Wynne v. Tufts University School of Medicine*, 1992). In order to obtain testing accommodations, students must first prove that they have disabilities that are in need of accommodations (*Argen v. New York State Board of Law Examiners*, 1994; *Pazer v. New York State Board of Law Examiners*, 1994). Further, students may be required to demonstrate that the requested modifications are actually related to their disabilities. In one case, a medical school student with dyslexia who had been given some testing accommodations was denied additional others. The Eighth Circuit affirmed that school officials in Iowa did all that was necessary to modify their testing procedures and that the student failed to show that the accommodations requested were actually related to his dyslexia (*Stern v. University of Osteopathic Medicine and Health Services*, 2000).

SUMMARY

Section 504 and the ADA are parallel laws that prohibit discrimination against individuals with disabilities in most educational institutions. Unlike the IDEA, neither Section 504 nor the ADA provides a funding mechanism to assist institutions in their nondiscrimination efforts. On the contrary, recipients of federal funds could lose significant federal resources by failing to comply with Section 504. Individuals do not need to prove that acts of discrimination were intentional in order to raise claims under Section 504 or the ADA.

Under Section 504 and the ADA, persons with impairments that adversely affect major life activities are considered to be individuals with disabilities. The impact of impairments must be permanent or long term in order to qualify as disabilities. Short-term or temporary impairments, such as a broken arm, that do not substantially limit major life activities do not meet the requirements for a disability under Section 504 or the ADA.

Mitigating measures may be taken into consideration in making determinations as to whether persons are individuals with disabilities covered by either statute. Mitigating measures could include devices, such as eyeglasses, that would substantially correct impairment. Further, inquiries into whether persons have disabilities must be individualized and fact specific. Impairments that may qualify as disabilities for one person may not do so for others. Moreover, inquiries must be situation-specific insofar as they may be disabilities under some circumstances but not others. It is up to individuals to notify institutions that they have impairments that may qualify for accommodations under Section 504.

In order to be covered under Section 504 or the ADA, individuals must be otherwise qualified to participate in institutions' programs and services. Generally, otherwise qualified means that individuals can meet minimum programmatic requirements and can participate in activities or benefits even though they have impairments. Impairments may be considered in evaluating whether individuals are otherwise qualified. For example, as was the situation in a case that came before the Supreme Court, a hearing-impaired person who relied on lip reading would not be otherwise qualified for a surgical nurse preparation program, because that person could not effectively communicate in an operating room where everyone wears surgical masks (*Southeastern Community College v. Davis*, 1979).

At the same time, officials must provide reasonable accommodations if doing so would allow individuals with disabilities to access or participate in programs and services that their institutions offer. Exactly what constitutes reasonable accommodations has been the subject of much litigation and, like determinations of disabilities themselves, must be fact-specific. Accommodations are not reasonable, in the school context, if they require educational institutions to lower their standards significantly or to make substantial modifications in their overall missions. In such circumstances, graduate school programs are not required to lower their minimum grade point average criteria for acceptance to accommodate students with disabilities who fail to meet these requirements. Further, accommodations that are excessively costly or that infringe on the rights of others are not required. For example, school officials would not be required to inoculate all staff members to accept students with contagious diseases if doing so would be prohibitively expensive or would go against the sincere religious beliefs of some staff members.

Figure 3.2 addresses frequently asked questions about students with disabilities.

RECOMMENDATIONS FOR PRACTICE

Governing boards of institutions of higher learning and educational officials should

- not exclude students with disabilities from educational institutions or deny them access to programs, benefits, or services solely because of their disabilities.
- when faced with discrimination claims under Section 504, evaluate whether students' disabilities are covered under Section 504, whether adverse decisions were made because of their disabilities, and whether individuals were otherwise qualified for the programs in question.

- not require students to show that acts of discrimination were intentional in order to maintain claims under Section 504 or the ADA.
- evaluate whether claimed impairments are permanent or long term.
- consider whether students are otherwise qualified by being able to meet the minimum requirements for the program with reasonable accommodations.
- individually assess students to determine whether they have impairments that qualify under Section 504 and the ADA.
- not subject students with disabilities to differential treatment solely because of their conditions or because they receive accommodations.
- note that Section 504 and the ADA do not require that all students with disabilities receive identical benefits; put another way, officials should consider all situations individually.
- address whether students require reasonable accommodations under Section 504 and the ADA to access a school's services and programs if they do not qualify for special education and related services under the IDEA.
- make sure that students with disabilities receive materials, teacher quality, length of school term, and daily hours of instruction comparable to what their peers receive.
- centralize services for students with disabilities as long as doing so does not effectively prevent students from participating in benefits or services.
- make individualized determinations regarding waivers of participation requirements for student-athletes with disabilities who may not meet usual requirements due to their disabilities or the effects of their disabilities.
- request medical clearance before allowing students with disabilities to participate in sports programs if they have reason to believe that students are at increased risk of injuries.
- provide accommodations unless doing so would create undue financial or administrative burdens.
- not make substantial modifications or fundamental alterations of programs and activities to provide accommodations if doing so would have a negative effect on the provision of other services to students with disabilities.
- make individualized inquiries into each student's situation before making decisions regarding reasonable accommodations.
- to the maximum extent possible, allow students with disabilities to address their conditions in school environments in the same manner that they address them elsewhere.

| Figure 3.2 | Frequently Asked Questions |

Q. When are students with disabilities otherwise qualified under Section 504 and the ADA?

A. Students with disabilities are otherwise qualified when they are eligible to participate in programs, activities, or benefits offered by the school in spite of their impairments. Otherwise qualified students must be permitted to take part in a school's benefits as long as it is possible for them to do so by means of reasonable accommodations. Once identified, otherwise qualified students are entitled to an appropriate public education, regardless of the nature or severity of their disabilities.

Q. What testing accommodations need to be given to students with disabilities?

A. Officials only need to provide students with testing accommodations that the students need due to their disabilities. The purpose of accommodations is to put these students on an equal footing with peers so that test results accurately reflect their abilities rather than the limitations imposed by their impairments. While officials may have to accommodate the manner in which examinations are administered, they need not change their content. For example, providing extra time for students with learning disabilities that affect how quickly they process information would be a reasonable accommodation, but giving them tests with less challenging items would not be required. In addition to extra time, the following are reasonable test accommodations that are commonly provided: a reader or a large-print version for a visually impaired student, a signer so that a hearing impaired student receives directions that are given to other students verbally, a scribe for a student with physical challenges, a less distracting environment for a student with attention deficit hyperactivity disorder, and frequent breaks for a student with chronic fatigue syndrome.

Q. Are students with disabilities exempt from eligibility rules for sports participation if the reasons why they failed to qualify are related to their disabilities?

A. Students with disabilities are not exempt from eligibility requirements, but waivers of some requirements may be required as long as the waivers do not put an excessive administrative burden on officials or give the student an unfair advantage. For instance, courts have held that rules that prohibit students over the age of 19 from participating in sports must be waived for students who repeated a grade due to their disabilities, but a waiver of the same rule might not be required if doing so would give unfair size or skill advantages to students with disabilities. As in all decisions involving students with disabilities, whether rules should be waived must be considered on an individualized basis.

Q. Are school officials required to put Section 504/ADA service plans in writing?

A. No. Even so, it is advisable to put plans in writing. Putting service plans in writing provides school officials with proper documentation both that they considered students' needs and that they acted to address their circumstances.

(Continued)

Figure 3.2 (Continued)

Q. What do students need to show to prove discrimination due to disabilities?

A. Students first need to show that they have disabilities as defined by Section 504 or the ADA. Second, students need to demonstrate that their impairments substantially limit a major life activity. In addition, students need to prove that school officials had knowledge of their disabilities and any accommodations they required. Finally, students need to show that officials took adverse actions against them solely because of their disabilities.

Q. Can school officials consider the mitigating effects of corrective measures when conducting individualized inquiries into students' situations?

A. Although the Supreme Court ruled that employers could consider the mitigating effects of corrective measures under the ADA, this issue has not been widely litigated in educational contexts involving students. It is likely that courts would not find students whose vision is corrected to 20/20 with glasses to be disabled under Section 504 or the ADA. However, it is unclear whether students who could take corrective measures but choose not to would still qualify as disabled. While most courts recognize that attention deficit hyperactivity disorder that adversely affects student learning is covered by Section 504 and the ADA, it is unclear whether those who could take medication to mitigate the effects of their conditions, but choose not to, would be protected.

REFERENCES

Albertson's, Inc. v. Kirkingburg, 527 U.S. 555 (1999).
Americans With Disabilities Act, 42 U.S.C. §§ 12101 *et seq.* (2005).
Argen v. New York State Board of Law Examiners, 860 F. Supp. 84 (W.D.N.Y. 1994).
Barnes v. Converse College, 436 F. Supp. 635 (D.S.C. 1977).
Barnett v. Fairfax County School Board, 721 F. Supp. 757 (E.D. Va. 1989), *affirmed,* 927 F.2d 146 (4th Cir. 1991).
Begay v. Hodel, 730 F. Supp. 1001 (D. Ariz. 1990).
Betts v. Rector and Visitors of the University of Virginia, 145 Fed. Appx. 7 (4th Cir. 2005).
Biank v. National Board of Medical Examiners, 130 F. Supp.2d 986 (N.D. Ill. 2000).
Bob Jones University v. United States, 461 U.S. 574 (1983).
Breen v. Charles R-IV School District, 2 F. Supp.2d 1214 (E.D. Mo. 1997).
Brookhart v. Illinois State Board of Education, 697 F.2d 179 (7th Cir. 1983).
Cave v. East Meadow Union Free School District, 480 F. Supp.2d 610 (E.D.N.Y. 2007).
Concerned Parents to Save Dreher Park Center v. City of West Palm Beach, 846 F. Supp. 986 (S.D. Fla. 1994).
Cordrey v. Euckert, 917 F.2d 1460 (6th Cir. 1990).
Costello v. Mitchell Public School District 79, 266 F.3d 916 (8th Cir. 2001).
Costello v. University of North Carolina at Greensboro, 394 F. Supp.2d 752 (M.D.N.C. 2005).

Crocker v. Tennessee Secondary School Athletic Association, 735 F. Supp. (M.D. Tenn. 1990), *affirmed without published opinion sub nom. Metropolitan Government of Nashville and Davidson County v. Crocker*, 908 F.2d 973 (6th Cir. 1990).

D'Amico v. New York State Board of Law Examiners, 813 F. Supp. 217 (W.D.N.Y. 1993).

Darian v. University of Massachusetts Boston, 980 F. Supp. 77 (D. Mass. 1997).

Doe v. Abington Friends School, 480 F.3d 252 (3d Cir. 2007).

Doe v. Dolton Elementary School District No. 148, 694 F. Supp. 440 (N.D. Ill. 1988).

Doe v. Eagle-Union Community School Corporation, 2 Fed Appx. 567 (7th Cir. 2001a), *certiorari denied*, 534 U.S. 1042 (2001b).

Easley v. Snider, 841 F. Supp. 668 (E.D. Pa. 1993).

El Kouni v. Trustees of Boston University, 169 F. Supp.2d 1 (D. Mass. 2001).

Ellis v. Morehouse School of Medicine, 925 F. Supp. 1529 (N.D. Ga. 1996).

Eric H. ex rel. John H. v. Methacton School District, 265 F. Supp.2d 513 (E.D. Pa. 2003).

Eva N. v. Brock, 741 F. Supp. 626 (E.D. Ky. 1990).

Falcone v. University of Minnesota, 388 F. Supp.2d 656 (8th Cir. 2004).

Gonzalez v. National Board of Medical Examiners, 60 F. Supp.2d 703 (E.D. Mich. 1999).

Halasz v. University of New England, 816 F. Supp. 37 (D. Me. 1993).

Hendricks v. Gilhool, 709 F. Supp. 1362 (E.D. Pa. 1989).

Hoot v. Milan Area Schools, 853 F. Supp. 243 (E.D. Mich. 1994).

Hornstine v. Township of Moorestown, 263 F. Supp.2d 887 (D.N.J. 2003).

Hunt v. St. Peter School, 963 F. Supp. 843 (W.D. Mo. 1997).

I. D. v. Westmoreland School District, 788 F. Supp. 634 (D.N.H. 1992).

Individuals with Disabilities Education Act, 20 U.S.C. §§ 1400 *et seq.* (2005).

J. D. v. Pawlett School District, 224 F.3d 60 (2d Cir. 2000).

Kaltenberger v. Ohio College of Podiatric Medicine, 162 F.3d 432 (6th Cir. 1998).

Knapp v. Northwestern University, 101 F.3d 473 (7th Cir. 1996).

Kohl v. Woodhaven Learning Center, 865 F.2d 930 (8th Cir. 1989).

Lane v. Pena, 867 F. Supp. 1050 (D.D.C. 1994).

Long v. Board of Education, District 128, 167 F. Supp.2d 988 (N.D. Ill. 2001).

McGregor v. Louisiana State University Board of Supervisors, 3 F.3d 850 (5th Cir. 1993).

McGuiness v. University of New Mexico School of Medicine, 170 F.3d 974 (10th Cir. 1998).

McPherson v. Michigan High School Athletic Association, 119 F.3d 453 (6th Cir. 1997).

Mershon v. St. Louis University, 442 F.3d 1069 (8th Cir. 2006).

Molly L. ex rel. B.L. v. Lower Merion School District, 194 F. Supp.2d 422 (E.D. Pa. 2002).

Moss v. Shelby County, 401 F. Supp.2d 850 (W.D. Tenn. 2005).

Murphy v. United Parcel Service, 527 U.S. 516 (1999).

No Child Left Behind Act, 20 U.S.C. §§ 6301 *et seq.* (2005).

Oberti v. Board of Education of the Borough of Clementon School District, 801 F. Supp. 1393 (D.N.J. 1992), *affirmed*, 995 F.2d 1204 (3d Cir. 1993).

Ohio Civil Rights Commission v. Case Western Reserve University, 666 N.E.2d 1376 (Ohio 1996).

Osborne, A. G., & Battaglino, L. (1996). Eligibility of students with disabilities for sports: Implications for policy. *Education Law Reporter, 105*, 379–388.

Pacella v. Tufts University School of Dental Medicine, 66 F. Supp.2d 234 (D. Mass. 1999).

Pahulu v. University of Kansas, 897 F. Supp. 1387 (D. Kan. 1995).

Pazer v. New York State Board of Law Examiners, 849 F. Supp. 284 (S.D.N.Y. 1994).

P. C. v. McLaughlin, 913 F.2d 1033 (2d Cir. 1990).

Petersen v. Hastings Public Schools, 831 F. Supp. 742 (D. Neb. 1993).

Pottgen v. Missouri State High School Activities Association, 40 F.3d 926 (8th Cir. 1994).

Powell v. National Board of Medical Examiners, 364 F.3d 79 (2d Cir. 2004).

Price v. National Board of Medical Examiners, 966 F. Supp.2d 419 (S.D. W.Va. 1997).

R. B. ex rel. L. B. v. Board of Education of the City of New York, 99 F. Supp.2d 411 (S.D.N.Y. 2000).

Rehabilitation Act, Section 504, 29 U.S.C. § 794 (2005).

Rush v. National Board of Medical Examiners, 268 F. Supp.2d 673 (N.D. Tex. 2003).

Russo, C. J., & Osborne, A. G. (2007). *Essential concepts and school-based cases in special education law.* Thousand Oaks, CA: Corwin Press.

St. Johnsbury Academy v. D.H., 240 F.3d 163 (2d Cir. 2001).

Singh v. George Washington University, 439 F. Supp.2d 8 (D.D.C. 2006).

Smith v. Special School District No. 1, 184 F.3d 764 (8th Cir. 1999).

Southeastern Community College v. Davis, 442 U.S. 397 (1979).

State of West Virginia ex rel. Lambert v. West Virginia State Board of Education, 447 S.E.2d 901 (W.Va. 1994).

Steere v. George Washington University, 439 F. Supp.2d 17 (D.D.C. 2006).

Stern v. University of Osteopathic Medicine and Health Services, 220 F.3d 906 (8th Cir. 2000).

Sullivan v. Vallejo City Unified School District, 731 F. Supp. 947 (E.D. Cal 1990).

Sutton v. United Air Lines, 527 U.S. 471 (1999).

Tatro v. State of Texas, 625 F.2d 557 (5th Cir. 1980), *on remand,* 516 F. Supp. 968 (N.D. Tex. 1981), *affirmed,* 703 F.2d 823 (5th Cir. 1983), *affirmed sub nom. Irving Independent School District v. Tatro,* 468 U.S. 883 (1984).

Thomas v. Atascadero Unified School District, 662 F. Supp. 376 (C.D. Cal. 1987).

Thomas v. Davidson Academy, 846 F. Supp. 611 (M.D. Tenn. 1994).

Tips v. Regents of Texas Tech University, 921 F. Supp. 1515 (N.D. Tex. 1996).

Toyota Motor Manufacturing v. Williams, 534 U.S. 184 (2002).

United States v. Board of Trustees for the University of Alabama, 908 F.2d 740 (11th Cir. 1990).

University Interscholastic League v. Buchanan, 848 S.W.2d 298 (Tex. App. Ct. 1993).

Villanueva v. Columbia University, 746 F. Supp. 297 (S.D.N.Y. 1990).

Walker v. District of Columbia, 157 F. Supp.2d 11 (D.D.C. 2001).

Weixel v. Board of Education of the City of New York, 287 F.3d 138 (2d Cir. 2002).

Wenger v. Canastota Central School District, 961 F. Supp. 416 (N.D.N.Y. 1997), *affirmed in part, vacated and remanded in part on other grounds,* 146 F.3d 123 (2d Cir. 1998).

White v. Denver Seminary, 157 F. Supp.2d 1171 (D. Colo. 2001).

Wong v. Regents of the University of California, 192 F.3d 807 (9th Cir. 1999).

Wynne v. Tufts University School of Medicine, 976 F.2d 791 (1st Cir. 1992).

Zukle v. Regents of the University of California, 166 F.3d 1041 (9th Cir. 1999).

4 Employees

INTRODUCTION

Federal law provides extensive protection for individuals with disabilities, including school employees under both Section 504 of the Rehabilitation Act of 1973 (Section 504, 2005) and the Americans With Disabilities Act (ADA, 2005). Section 504, which covers students, school employees, and others who may be in schools, applies to those who have, who had, or who are believed to have had impairments that significantly impact on major life activities identified in Chapter 2. Individuals who are otherwise qualified, meaning that they are qualified to participate in activities despite their impairments, cannot be denied the benefits of, or participation in, programs that receive federal financial assistance as long as they can do so by means of reasonable accommodations (34 C.F.R. § 104.12). However, as noted below, school boards may also be able to apply defenses in some situations.

Title I of the ADA prohibits discrimination by private sector employers with 15 or more employees. Title II of the act applies to public accommodations such as schools in language similar to that of Section 504, requiring reasonable accommodations for otherwise qualified individuals. The result is that plaintiffs use the ADA extensively in cases alleging employment discrimination just as disputes involving students are increasingly being filed under Section 504.

The ADA exceeds the coverage of Section 504 insofar as it specifically addresses the preemployment rights of individuals with disabilities (42 U.S.C. § 12112(d)(2)). The ADA's provisions prohibit school officials and other employers from inquiring about the type, nature, and severity of impairments of job applicants, but employers may ask about their ability to perform job-related tasks. Moreover, once officials have offered applicants jobs, they can condition hiring on submission to medical examinations as long as all prospective employees must do so. Still, the ADA forbids school boards from requiring current employees to submit to medical examinations about the nature of their disabilities unless they can prove that doing so is job related (42 U.S.C. § 12112(d)(4)).

When otherwise qualified employees allege discrimination based on disabilities, whether under Section 504 or the ADA, employers must make reasonable accommodations unless they can assert one of three defenses. Put another way, when school boards and officials, whether in public or nonpublic schools, act as employers, they can avoid compliance if making accommodations would result in "a fundamental alteration in the nature of [a] program" (*Southeastern Community College v. Davis* [*Davis*], 1979, p. 410); if they impose "undue financial burden[s]" (*Davis* at p. 412); or if the presence of individuals with disabilities creates a substantial risk of injury to themselves or others (*School Board of Nassau County, Florida v. Arline* [*Arline*], 1987).

The Supreme Court first applied Section 504 in a K–12 setting in *Arline* when it affirmed that school officials violated a teacher's rights by terminating her employment due to recurrences of tuberculosis. In ruling that the teacher was otherwise qualified for the job, the Court enunciated a four-part test for use in cases involving contagious diseases. These four elements address the nature of a risk, its duration, its severity, and the probabilities that the disease will be transmitted and will cause varying degrees of harm. On remand, a federal trial court in Florida agreed that since the teacher was otherwise qualified, she was entitled to reinstatement and back pay, typical remedies in such litigation under Section 504 and the ADA.

Based on the significance that Section 504 has for educational institutions in their capacity as employers, this chapter, which examines illustrative cases from the vast amount of litigation involving employees, is divided into three substantive sections. These sections address discrimination claims, what it means to be otherwise qualified, and reasonable accommodations. The chapter rounds out with a brief conclusion before offering practical recommendations for educational leaders.

In reviewing representative litigation from among the many cases filed pursuant to Section 504 and the ADA, it is important to note that since many of the disputes can fit under more than one category because they involve related issues, some are used under more than one heading. Insofar as this chapter is concerned with the rights of educational employees with disabilities, it cites a variety of cases that arose in noneducational contexts, since the implications of these decisions apply in educational settings.

DISCRIMINATION CLAIMS

In order to maintain discrimination claims in educational and other employment contexts under Section 504 and the ADA, employees must first file their suits within the appropriate statues of limitations, discussed in greater detail in Chapter 6, as controlled by analogous state disability laws (*Putkowski v. Warwick Valley Central School District*, 2005).

Differential Treatment

Once plaintiffs have established that their suits can proceed, they must be able to demonstrate that they were treated differently than staff members who were not impaired or that educational officials made adverse employment decisions based on their impairments. For example, a federal trial court in Ohio rejected the Section 504 claim of a part-time instructional aide with a disability who alleged that officials discriminated against him when he was laid off after he worked the maximum number of hours allowed for part-time staff (*Spells v. Cuyahoga Community College*, 1994). The court explained that the plaintiff's claim could not proceed, since part-time employees who were not impaired were laid off for the same reason.

In another case, a former high school principal in Kansas, who was a recovering alcoholic, was unable to show that a school board discriminated against him under Section 504 when it abolished his position and did not appoint him to the newly created job of combined elementary and high school principal (*Pierce v. Engle*, 1989). The court found that the board had not discriminated against the plaintiff, because it acted based on legitimate economic reasons. The court observed that the board acted with good cause in combining the two jobs and offering the new position to the former elementary principal, because he was certified for grades kindergarten through 12, a qualification that the former high school principal lacked.

> Plaintiffs must be able to demonstrate that they were treated differently than staff members who were not impaired or that educational officials made adverse employment decisions based on individuals' impairments.

Employees with disabilities cannot proceed with discrimination claims if they lack the skills to perform jobs even if they receive reasonable accommodations. In such circumstances courts typically rule in favor of school officials, as long as the officials can demonstrate that they made what amounted to adverse employment decisions with regard to employees with disabilities for nondiscriminatory reasons. In one such case, the federal trial court in Washington, D.C., was of the opinion that a division of the federal Department of Education did not discriminate under Section 504 against an employee who had quadriplegic cerebral palsy since birth, a condition that limited his control of his hands, arms, and legs (*Adrain v. Alexander*, 1992). Additionally, the plaintiff used a wheelchair, was physically unable to write legibly, and was difficult to understand when he spoke. The court was satisfied that officials were able to demonstrate that the plaintiff was denied the promotion because his work performance was neither up to standards nor had it improved after he was provided with accommodations.

Impairments Not Covered

Courts usually reject discrimination claims if alleged employee disabilities are not covered by Section 504 or the ADA. In an illustrative case, the federal trial court in Maine interpreted the term "individual with disabilities" as not including a man with sexual behavior disorders (*Winston v. Maine Technical College System*, 1993). After an instructor was dismissed for violating his college's sexual harassment policy, he unsuccessfully alleged that his employment was wrongfully terminated, because he had a sexual addiction that was a mental disability under Section 504. Similarly, a federal trial court in New York pointed out that a faculty member in a law school who suffered a stroke was not discriminated against when he received smaller salary raises than colleagues (*Redlich v. Albany Law School of Union University*, 1995). The court asserted that the plaintiff was not disabled as defined by Section 504, since his stroke had not substantially limited a major life activity. In addition, the court noted that the reasons why the faculty member's salary raise was not comparable to those of his colleagues were related to his overall job performance.

In order to be actionable, impairment must have permanent or long-term effects under Section 504 or the ADA. The Supreme Court, in a noneducation case, *Toyota Motor Manufacturing v. Williams* (2002), emphasized that an impairment must prevent or severely restrict an individual from engaging in activities that are of central importance

> Courts usually reject discrimination claims if alleged employee disabilities are not covered by Section 504 or the ADA.

to most people's daily lives to be a disability. The Court stressed that the impact of an impairment must be permanent or long term.

Mitigation of Impairments

The U.S. Supreme Court has handed down three decisions that, when taken together, indicate that impairments are not disabilities under the ADA if they can be mitigated. These cases were discussed thoroughly in Chapter 3 but are briefly summarized here. In the first case, *Sutton v. United Airlines* (1999), the Court stated that when individuals take measures to correct for or mitigate impairments, the effects of those measures must be considered when evaluating whether the persons are substantially limited in major life activities. In other words, individuals whose physical or mental impairments are corrected through medication or other measures do not have impairments that presently limit major life activities. In the second dispute, *Murphy v. United Parcel Service* (1999), the Court added that consideration of whether an individual's impairment substantially limits one or more major life activities is to be made in view of the mitigating measures that an individual uses. In the final suit, *Albertson's, Inc. v. Kirkingburg* (1999), the Court announced that it does not matter whether corrective measures are undertaken with artificial aids, such as medication or devices, or via the body's own systems, such as learning to adapt to or compensate for impairments.

In the first of three more recent disputes, the Fifth Circuit affirmed that since the depression that a school psychologist in Texas suffered from was treatable by medication, she was not an otherwise qualified individual who was covered by the ADA after her school board refused to renew her employment contract (*Winters v. Pasadena Independent School District*, 2005). A year earlier, a federal trial court in New York rejected a teacher's claim that her systemic lupus erythematosus was a physical impairment that entitled her to protection under the ADA (*Temple v. Board of Education of*

City of New York, 2004). The court remarked that because the condition did not substantially limit a major life function, the ADA was inapplicable. Further, a federal trial court in Georgia was of the view that since a plaintiff's impairment did not limit her ability to perform a broad class of jobs, specifically teaching, even though it might have interfered with her current job working in a day care center, she was not covered by the ADA (*Stockton v. World of Hope Daycare,* 2007).

Disciplinary Action

Employers are permitted to take appropriate disciplinary action against employees who commit egregious or criminal misconduct, regardless of whether they are disabled. For instance, the Sixth Circuit upheld the dismissal of a coach who had been arrested for driving under the influence of alcohol and public intoxication (*Maddox v. University of Tennessee,* 1995). The court posited that university officials could expect that the coach, who was an alcoholic, conform to the same performance and behavior standards as other employees, even though his unsatisfactory job performance had been due to his alcoholism. Other courts have agreed that employees can be dismissed for excessive absenteeism even if their having missed work was related to their disabilities, because being present is an essential requirement of most jobs (*Linares v. City of White Plains,* 1991; *Walders v. Garrett,* 1991).

OTHERWISE QUALIFIED INDIVIDUALS WITH DISABILITIES

On two occasions, in *Arline* and *Davis,* the Supreme Court ruled that individuals with disabilities are otherwise qualified if they can perform all essential requirements of their positions in spite of their impairments. In addition, as highlighted by a noneducation case from the District of Columbia, employees must be able to complete assigned tasks within a reasonable period of time (*Carr v. Reno,* 1994). If individuals are unable to perform essential job functions, even with reasonable accommodations, then courts agree that they are not otherwise qualified under Section 504 or the ADA.

Essential Job Functions

It almost goes without saying that an essential requirement of most positions, especially in school systems, is regular attendance. To this end, employees who are unable to attend the workplace in a reliable and predictable manner are not otherwise qualified. As reflected by the first of two cases from Pennsylvania, a federal trial court asserted that Section 504 does not protect excessive absenteeism, even when it is caused by a variety of illnesses that include time to recover from surgery (*Santiago v. Temple University*, 1990). More recently, the Third Circuit affirmed that a school board in Pennsylvania did not violate Section 504 when it refused to accommodate a teacher with a kidney disease that caused her to suffer chronic abdominal pain and fatigue (*Kurek v. North Allegheny School District*, 2007). According to the court, since completion of a full work day is an essential function of a teacher's job, the plaintiff was not an otherwise qualified individual who was entitled to the protection of Section 504.

A related job requirement is that classroom teachers are expected to be present physically in classrooms and to interact appropriately with students (*Mustafa v. Clark County School District*, 1998). Teachers whose disabilities render them unable to interact with children may not be entitled to assignments that do not involve sustained contact with large groups of students. Even so, insofar as classroom teaching is generally considered to be an essential function of a teacher's job, the inability to teach in classrooms in most situations means that individuals cannot meet all of the requirements of being teachers in spite of their impairments.

> An essential requirement of most positions, especially in school systems, is regular attendance.

Further litigation illustrates issues that arise about the ability of teachers, or more properly, their lack thereof, to interact with students. In a case from New Hampshire that was filed pursuant to the ADA, the federal trial court declared that school board officials did not have to make the accommodations that a teacher with ADHD requested (*Hess v. Rochester School District*, 2005). The court was convinced that if school board officials had granted the teacher's request that he be permitted to calm students by allowing them to listen to music and play games for up to half of the time that they were supposed to be in class, he would not have been performing the essential function of instructing students. In a similar dispute, the federal trial court in Kansas rejected the claim of a teacher who was significantly hearing-impaired after his school board refused to hire a full-time classroom aide to help him to preserve classroom discipline (*Henry v. Unified School District*, 2004). The court commented that since being able to discipline students was an essential job function, providing the teacher with an aide was not a reasonable accommodation under the ADA.

Reassignments

If nonclassroom positions are available, teachers may be entitled to reassignments to one of those jobs. For example, the Ninth Circuit decided that where a teacher in Nevada suffered from depression, posttraumatic stress disorder, and panic attacks, the school board had to grant his reasonable request that he be accommodated by being placed in a nonteaching position, since it was feasible to do so (*Mustafa v. Clark County School District,* 1998).

In a case dealing with a school custodian, the Supreme Court of Montana, relying on Section 504's regulations and state law, determined that a school board acted improperly in refusing to reinstate a custodian with a back injury (*Butterfield v. Sidney Public Schools,* 2001). The court thought that since the custodian was "physically disabled" within the meaning of state law, board officials had to assign him to a position that would not require him to engage in heavy lifting.

Failure to Meet Prerequisite Requirements

Failure to meet teacher certification requirements may disqualify individuals even if their inability to meet such standards is allegedly due to their disabilities. The Fourth Circuit reasoned that a teacher in Virginia who claimed to have a learning disability and had not passed the communications portion of the National Teachers Examination after numerous attempts was not otherwise qualified for teacher certification (*Pandazides v. Virginia Board of Education,* 1992, 1994). The court recognized that the skills measured by the communications portion of the examination were necessary for competent performance as a classroom teacher. The court concluded that the teacher was not otherwise qualified, because she could not demonstrate that she could perform essential job functions. More than a decade later, a federal trial court in New York rejected the ADA claim of a teacher who refused to take a certification examination after officials failed to accommodate her dyslexia. The court ruled that the teacher's claim could not proceed, because in choosing not to take the examination, she demonstrated that she was not otherwise qualified for the job (*Falchenberg v. New York City Department of Education,* 2005).

Another qualification that is essential for educators is being able to write. In one case, a federal trial court in New York rejected the claim of a school counselor with the learning disabilities of dyslexia and dysgraphia, which impacted her ability to write (*Hanig v. Yorktown Central School District,* 2005). In granting the school board's motion to dismiss the claim, the court acknowledged that since the counselor resigned rather than face the prospect of being denied tenure, her claim that educational officials violated her rights under the ADA when they informed a possible employer about her lack of writing ability did not qualify as retaliation under the law.

Their disabilities aside, educational officials can expect individuals to be able to perform their duties in a safe manner. In such a case, admittedly in a nonschool setting, the Fifth Circuit affirmed that a city in Texas did not discriminate under Section 504 and state law in dismissing an employee with Parkinson's disease, since officials demonstrated that his lack of balance due to his illness meant that he was no longer otherwise qualified to perform his job safely (*Chiari v. City of League City*, 1991). Further, in a case from Ohio, the Sixth Circuit affirmed that a school board had not discriminated under the ADA in refusing to hire a bus driver who had been involved in an earlier beer-drinking incident at an elementary school (*Martin v. Barnesville Exempted Village School District Board of Education*, 2000). The court pointed out that the prior incident provided the board with a legitimate, non-discriminatory reason for not hiring the driver.

When dealing with employees who consume alcohol, it is important to keep in mind that the ADA permits school boards and other employers to develop policies that prohibit employees from the illegal use of alcohol (and drugs) in the workplace (42 U.S.C. § 12114(c)). In addition, the ADA specifically permits school boards and other employers to test "transportation employees" for on-duty impairments for alcohol and illegal drug use (42 U.S.C. § 12114(3)). Safety concerns aside, the ADA probably protects recovering alcoholics (and drug users) who can demonstrate that they have been able to avoid performance-impairing substances. Along this line of thought, the federal trial court in Minnesota rejected a former school janitor's claim of alcoholism, since he had been sober for 16 years (*Boyer v. KRS Computer and Business School*, 2001).

In a related concern, bus drivers who are poorly controlled diabetics are not otherwise qualified, since they pose an unpredictable risk of developing hypoglycemia or the complications of hypoglycemia in the performance of their duties insofar as adverse health reactions may include a sudden loss of vision or consciousness while operating vehicles (*Wood v. Omaha School District*, 1994). On the other hand, if diabetes can be controlled and bus drivers' fitness to operate vehicles easily monitored, employees can be considered otherwise qualified (*Commonwealth, Department of Transportation, Bureau of Driver Licensing v. Tinsley*, 1989). The same would be true for drivers who have other medical conditions such as a seizure disorder (*Commonwealth, Department of Transportation, Bureau of Driver Licensing v. Chalfant*, 1989). To the extent that transportation employees must be individually assessed for fitness to perform their job duties, this is a good example of when boards could require periodic physical examinations of drivers under the ADA in order to ensure student safety.

A federal trial court in Ohio, in a nonschool case, in essentially borrowing from the four-part test that the Supreme Court enunciated in *Arline* in dealing with contagious diseases, found that before refusing to hire individuals with disabilities due to perceived risks, school officials must determine the nature, duration, and severity of the risk; the probability that the potential injury will actually occur; and the possibility that reasonable modifications of policies, practices, or procedures will mitigate the risks (*Bombrys v. City of Toledo*, 1993). In this case, the court permanently enjoined city officials from implementing blanket exclusion for persons with insulin-dependent diabetes from employment as police officers where there was no evidence that the applicant in question was unable to perform essential job functions.

Poor Performance and Misconduct

Section 504 and the ADA do not protect incompetent employees or those who exhibit poor performance. A federal trial court in New York upheld a school board's dismissal of a custodian who suffered from narcolepsy and sleep apnea (*Sanzo v. Uniondale Union Free School District*, 2005). The court agreed that the board did not violate the ADA in terminating the custodian's employment, because rather than refer to his illness, officials articulated legitimate nondiscriminatory reasons for his dismissal, namely his poor performance and misconduct in 15 of 19 areas in which he was evaluated.

Section 504 and the ADA also do not protect employees who commit acts of misconduct, even when their behavior can be attributed to their disabilities. In one noneducation case, a special agent of the Alcohol, Tobacco, and Firearms Agency of the federal government lost his job because he was involved in a vehicular homicide while intoxicated (*Wilber v. Brady*, 1992). The court rejected the agent's proffered defense that he was an alcoholic, because it was a condition that disqualified him from being an otherwise qualified individual with a disability under Section 504.

In another case, an appellate court in California upheld the dismissal of an alcoholic employee who repeatedly reported to work while intoxicated and was unable to perform his duties (*Gonzalez v. California State Personnel Board*, 1995). The court wrote that since the employee was dismissed because of his misconduct, not his alcoholism, relief was unavailable under Section 504. Similarly, an appellate court in Connecticut upheld the dismissal of a teacher who had been arrested and charged with possession of cocaine (*Gedney v. Board of Education of the Town of Groton*, 1997). The court maintained that the former teacher's criminal conduct undermined his ability to work as an educator.

REASONABLE ACCOMMODATIONS

Under Section 504 and the ADA, employers must provide reasonable accommodations so that otherwise qualified employees with disabilities can work and compete with their colleagues who are not impaired (*Fink v. New York City Department of Personnel*, 1994). The purpose of providing accommodations is so that employees with disabilities can lead normal lives (*McWright v. Alexander*, 1992), not that they be given special advantages. Accommodations may include alterations to the physical environment, adjustments to work schedules, or minor changes in the job responsibilities. Conditions that qualify as reasonable accommodations have been the subject of a great deal of litigation.

Employers are not required to make accommodations if doing so would place undue burdens on their operations. At the same time, courts do not usually treat minor accommodations as excessively burdensome. For instance, an appellate court in Pennsylvania observed that monitoring a diabetic's ability to operate a school bus on a daily basis did not place an undue burden on the school system (*Commonwealth, Department of Transportation, Bureau of Driver Licensing v. Tinsley*, 1989).

> Employers are not required to make accommodations if doing so would place undue burdens on their operations.

As reflected by a case from Wisconsin, the burden of proof that requested accommodations would create an undue financial or administrative burden for their institution generally rests on educational officials (*Byrne v. Board of Education, School District of West Allis–West Milwaukee*, 1990). In other words, officials must prove that employees or applicants are unfit rather than having individuals demonstrate that they are eligible to perform job duties.

Accommodating Physical Challenges

A federal trial court in New York rejected a school board's motion to dismiss the Section 504 and ADA claims of a teacher with multiple sclerosis who alleged that its proffered justification for terminating her employment—that her job performance for the past three years had been unsatisfactory, after she served more than 20 years with the district—was a pretext for disability discrimination. The court noted that since issues of fact remained as to whether officials reasonably accommodated the teacher by allowing her to take rest periods during the day and to transfer to a school closer to home so that she could perform essential job functions, it was unable to grant a motion to dismiss her claim under

Section 504 and the ADA (*Young v. Central Square Central School District*, 2002). In a case that reached the merits of the underlying claim, the Ninth Circuit reversed an earlier judgment in favor of a school board on behalf of an injured groundskeeper whose employment it had terminated (*Johnson v. Paradise Valley Unified School District*, 2001). According to the court, there was sufficient evidence to support a jury's verdict that school officials regarded the groundskeeper as disabled under the ADA.

As teaching staffs age, disputes arise concerning the conditions of employees with arthritis. In the first of two cases, the federal trial court in Maryland rejected a school board's motion for summary judgment under both Section 504 and state law where a teacher with rheumatoid arthritis filed suit, claiming that officials discriminated against her on the job when she requested a room change. The court refused the board's motion, since it was of the opinion that there was a triable issue of fact as to whether the teacher could perform her job and whether officials accommodated her request (*Ross v. Board of Education of Prince George's County*, 2002). In a second case involving arthritis, the federal trial court in the District of Columbia reached a like result (*Gordon v. District of Columbia*, 2007). The court pointed out that since a retired teacher's degenerative arthritis, which required her to walk with the aid of a cane, was an impairment under both Section 504 and the ADA, there was no ground on which to grant the board's motion to dismiss the plaintiff's claim that school officials failed to accommodate her reasonable requests, including that she be granted access to an accessible bathroom, that she be given keys to locked emergency doors, and that shelves she could no longer reach be lowered to accommodate her.

In another case involving walking, the federal trial court in Maryland granted a school board's motion for summary judgment in the face of an ADA claim filed by a special education teacher whose contract was not renewed after she received a negative evaluation (*Stewart v. Weast*, 2002). The court posited that since not being able to walk long distances or climb stairs did not substantially limit the teacher's ability to perform her job, she failed to establish that she was disabled under the ADA. The court added that officials accommodated the plaintiff by giving her an elevator key, freeing her from teaching for the last period of the day, and recommending that she teach only a half-day schedule so as to avoid having to change classrooms.

Another issue over which the courts are split is whether employees who are overweight are otherwise qualified individuals who are entitled to accommodations. On the one hand, the First Circuit affirmed that under Section 504, a job applicant who was diagnosed as "morbidly obese" was entitled to a trial on the merits to consider whether a residential facility for the mentally retarded discriminated against her in not offering her a job (*Cook v. State of Rhode Island, Department of Mental Health, Retardation, and Hospitals,* 1993). The court indicated that whether the applicant suffered from an immutable condition was a question of fact for a jury to consider in evaluating whether her condition was an impairment that qualified her for protection under Section 504. However, a federal trial court in Virginia reached the opposite result in holding that a trooper who was reclassified to a job as a dispatcher because she was overweight was not otherwise qualified for her job under Section 504. The court declared that because the plaintiff lacked the skills to protect herself from assault and to pursue, confront, and capture offenders, the decision of her superiors to reclassify her was rationally related to her ability to perform or not perform expected job duties, and she was not protected by Section 504 (*Smaw v. Commonwealth of Virginia Department of State Police,* 1994).

Courts are also split on carpal tunnel syndrome. The Ninth Circuit reversed in favor of a janitor in Nevada who alleged that a school board violated his rights by not offering him the reasonable accommodation of making him a school safety officer before terminating his employment (*Wellington v. Lyon County School District,* 1999). Conversely, a federal trial court in Connecticut rejected the claim of a part-time employee that a school board refused to hire her for a full-time job in light of her charge that officials discriminated against her due to her disability. The court did not think that carpal tunnel syndrome substantially limited her major life activity of working (*Cutler v. Hamden Board of Education,* 2001).

Accommodating Disease and Illness

As with other diseases, courts reached mixed results in disputes involving cancer. The federal trial court in New Mexico permitted the claim of a former school administrator with breast cancer to proceed under both Section 504 and the ADA (*Keller v. Board of Education of City of Albuquerque,* 2001). Yet, a court in Missouri disagreed in refusing to treat cancer as a disabling impairment (*Treiber v. Lindbergh School District,* 2002). Moreover, an appellate court in New York, relying only partly on state law, affirmed that school officials had not discriminated against a teacher who had cancer surgery due to her condition, since her illness had not limited a major life activity (*Sirota v. New York City Board of Education,* 2001). The court contended that the teacher's illness did not entitle her to an accommodation.

In the only case directly involving the rights of a school employee with AIDS/HIV, a teacher successfully challenged his school board's refusal to reinstate him to his job due to his illness. Reversing in favor of the teacher, and granting his request for an injunction, the Ninth Circuit was of the view that school officials violated the teacher's rights under Section 504 (*Chalk v. United States District Court, Central District of California*, 1988). The court remarked that there was no adequate medical evidence that he would have passed the disease on to his students or coworkers, and public fear of AIDS was not sufficient grounds to deny his request that it order school officials to permit him to return to his job.

Reassignments

Employers are not required to make accommodations that would essentially change the nature of employees' jobs, nor are they necessarily required to reassign employees with disabilities to other positions. Even so, employers may have to reassign individuals who are unable to perform essential job functions with reasonable accommodations if there exist, or soon will exist, vacant positions that they are able to perform (*Ransom v. State of Arizona Board of Regents*, 1997).

In situations involving classroom teachers, as reflected by a case from Nevada that reached the Ninth Circuit, a school board was required to reassign an individual who was otherwise qualified to a nonteaching role, since it had such positions in the district (*Mustafa v. Clark County School District*, 1998). However, educational officials cannot be required to reassign personnel when there is no other position available for which employees are qualified (*Black v. Frank*, 1990). Further, in a dispute that was resolved entirely on the basis of state law, an appellate court in Washington affirmed that a school board's refusal to reassign a teacher with anxiety disorder to another school did not violate a statutory requirement that it make reasonable accommodations for individuals with disabilities (*Wilson v. Wenatchee School District*, 2002). The court agreed with the board that reassigning the teacher to a school where he would have worked with a different principal was not a reasonable accommodation.

A case from Texas, albeit not in an educational context, illustrates the principle that employers are also not required to create new positions or accommodate employees with disabilities by eliminating essential aspects of their current positions (*Alexander v. Frank*, 1991). In granting their motion for summary judgment, a federal trial court maintained that Section 504 did not obligate officials of the postal service to create a new position for a worker who was identified as totally disabled, since she was not otherwise qualified to work.

As noted earlier, regular attendance is considered to be an essential requirement of most jobs. To this end, the federal trial court in Maryland specified that county officials were not required to allow a firefighter with asthma to work only when his condition allowed him to do so, because this would have meant that he was not otherwise qualified for the job (*Huber v. Howard County*, 1994). Further, a federal trial court in Virginia determined that a requested accommodation of being allowed to work when the employee's illness permitted would result in an undue hardship to the employer (*Walders v. Garrett*, 1991). On the other hand, the federal trial court in Maryland was satisfied that a school board adequately accommodated a plaintiff whose illness caused frequent absences when it hired a long-term substitute to work alongside the teacher (*Nichols v. Harford County Board of Education*, 2002).

Relief Denied

As is revealed in the following cases, courts have denied relief in a variety of circumstances. The Fifth Circuit ruled in favor of a school board in Mississippi in a suit by a teacher whose contract was not renewed (*Gammage v. West Jasper School Board of Education*, 1999). The court conceded that school officials knew of the teacher's disability, but she failed to prove that it caused her to have any work-related limitations needing accommodations. The Sixth Circuit affirmed that a disruptive tenured teacher in Michigan failed to prove that he was disabled under the ADA and state law after he refused to undergo psychological testing (*Sullivan v. River Valley School District*, 1999). The court acknowledged that the board had the authority to suspend the teacher, since his behavior gave the board a reasonable basis to check on his ability to continue working.

The federal trial court in Minnesota rejected a former school janitor's claim of schizophrenia, because his illness did not substantially limit a major life function; in addition, the court rejected a claim of alcoholism, since the employee was sober for 16 years (*Boyer v. KRS Computer and Business School*, 2001). The federal trial court in Kansas rejected claims by an employee who sought to perform only light duties on the ground that such a request was not reasonable (*Hinson v. U.S.D. No. 500*, 2002). Further, in New York, a federal trial court rejected a teacher's ADA claim on the ground that high blood pressure is not a disability, because it could have been mitigated with medication (*Ramirez v. New York City Board of Education*, 2007). The court also commented that epilepsy and depression did not substantially impair the plaintiff's ability to teach.

SUMMARY

Together, Section 504 and the ADA provide extensive protections from discrimination for otherwise qualified educational (and other) employees as well as job applicants with disabilities as defined by these statutes. In essence, educational employers cannot take adverse action against employees, treat employees differently, or refuse to hire applicants on the basis of their disabilities. If individuals with disabilities are capable of performing essential job functions, then employers must afford them the same opportunities to fill those positions as persons who are not disabled.

Persons are otherwise qualified for jobs if they are capable of performing all essential job functions with reasonable accommodations. Under this mandate, employers are not required to provide accommodations that would be overly expensive or that would create undue administrative burdens. Considering this, school officials might be required to locate the classrooms of teachers with physical impairments on a first floor but would not be required to hire a personal aide to accompany that educator throughout the day. Figure 4.1 provides some examples of interview questions that are and are not appropriate with respect to disabilities, while Figure 4.2 addresses some frequently asked questions about employees with disabilities.

Figure 4.1   Interview Questions

Examples of Inappropriate Interview Questions	Examples of Appropriate Interview Questions
Do you have a disability?	Are you able to perform the essential functions of this job as outlined in the job description?
Do you have any medical conditions?	Will you be able to carry out all of the requirements of this position in a safe manner?
Do you have any physical limitations?	One requirement of this position is to frequently carry heavy boxes. Are you able to carry 50 pounds for a short distance?
How many sick days did you use during the last year of your past job?	Will you be able to report to work on time on a regular basis?

RECOMMENDATIONS FOR PRACTICE

School boards and educational leaders should

- maintain accurate, up-to-date, and detailed job descriptions for all positions.
- try to identify in advance the types of accommodations that boards can afford to make in light of the financial implications that such changes might engender; for example, it is one thing to allow individuals to transfer or work on a part-time basis but may be something altogether different to call for job restructuring.
- prepare interviewers to be sensitive to and deal with the needs of applicants who are impaired.
- ensure that compliance officers regularly monitor or audit educational programming to be certain that it complies with the dictates of Section 504, the ADA, and other applicable federal and state laws.
- require medical exams for all prospective employees to determine fitness for employment, especially those in child- or safety-sensitive positions, not just those with known disabilities.
- change the schedules of employees with disabilities to accommodate them if doing so does not present an undue burden.
- be prepared to transfer employees with disabilities to other positions, if such positions exist and are available, as a reasonable accommodation.
- prepare checklists to help ensure that staff members are responding to employee requests for accommodation in a timely and appropriate manner.
- take steps to ensure that staff members with disabilities are not subjected to differential treatment because of their disabilities or because of their need for accommodations.
- provide regular professional development sessions for all professional staff and board members to help them have a better understanding of how their legal systems operate and, more specifically, to recognize the significant differences and interplay between and among Section 504, the ADA, and other federal and state disability-related laws so as to better serve the needs of employees with disabilities.
- recognize that in light of the complexity of disability law, it is important to rely on the advice of attorneys who specialize in education law, especially on the rights of the disabled; if school officials are unable to find such attorneys on their own, they should contact their state school boards associations, bar associations, or professional groups such as the Education Law Association or National School Boards Association.

Figure 4.2   Frequently Asked Questions

Q. What employment activities are covered by Section 504 and the ADA?

A. Section 504 and the ADA prohibit discrimination in all phases of employment, including application procedures, hiring, promotions, and termination. In addition, Section 504 and the ADA apply to job training, compensation and fringe benefits, layoffs, and tenure.

Q. Who is protected by Section 504 and the ADA?

A. Qualified individuals with disabilities are protected by the terms of Section 504 and the ADA. Individuals with disabilities are those who have physical or mental impairments that substantially limit one or more major life activities, who have a record of such impairments, or who are regarded as having impairments.

Q. What does it mean to be otherwise qualified?

A. In the employment context the term *otherwise qualified* means that persons are able to perform all job functions in spite of the disability. Thus, individuals who have all of the necessary qualifications and can perform the essential functions of the position with reasonable accommodations are otherwise qualified.

Q. What is a reasonable accommodation?

A. A reasonable accommodation is a modification to a position or a work setting that allows qualified persons to perform essential job functions. It does not require employers to make any accommodations that would present undue financial or administrative hardships. For example, employers are not required to assign major job functions to other employees. Similarly, employers need not lower quality standards to accommodate employees with disabilities.

REFERENCES

Adrain v. Alexander, 792 F. Supp. 124 (D.D.C. 1992).
Albertson's, Inc. v. Kirkingburg, 527 U.S. 555 (1999).
Alexander v. Frank, 777 F. Supp. 516 (N.D. Tex. 1991).
Americans With Disabilities Act, 42 U.S.C. §§ 12101 *et seq.* (2005).
Black v. Frank, 730 F. Supp. 1087 (S.D. Ala. 1990).
Bombrys v. City of Toledo, 849 F. Supp. 1210 (N.D. Ohio 1993).
Boyer v. KRS Computer and Business School, 171 F. Supp.2d 950 (D. Minn. 2001).
Butterfield v. Sidney Public Schools, 32 P.3d 1243 (Mont. 2001).
Byrne v. Board of Education, School District of West Allis–West Milwaukee, 741 F. Supp.
    167 (E.D. Wis. 1990).
Carr v. Reno, 23 F.3d 525 (D.C. Cir. 1994).
Chalk v. United States District Court, Central District of California, 840 F.2d 701 (9th
    Cir. 1988).
Chiari v. City of League City, 920 F.2d 311 (5th Cir. 1991).
Code of Federal Regulations, as cited.

Commonwealth, Department of Transportation, Bureau of Driver Licensing v. Chalfant, 565 A.2d 1252 (Pa. Commw. Ct. 1989).

Commonwealth, Department of Transportation, Bureau of Driver Licensing v. Tinsley, 564 A.2d 286 (Pa. Commw. Ct. 1989).

Cook v. State of Rhode Island, Department of Mental Health, Retardation, and Hospitals, 10 F.3d 17 (1st Cir. 1993).

Cutler v. Hamden Board of Education, 150 F. Supp.2d 356 (D. Conn. 2001).

Falchenberg v. New York City Department of Education, 375 F. Supp.2d 344 (S.D.N.Y. 2005).

Fink v. New York City Department of Personnel, 855 F. Supp. 69 (S.D.N.Y. 1994).

Gammage v. West Jasper School Board of Education, 179 F.3d 952 (5th Cir. 1999).

Gedney v. Board of Education of the Town of Groton, 703 A.2d 804 (Conn. Ct. App. 1997).

Gonzalez v. California State Personnel Board, 39 Cal. Rptr.2d 282 (Cal. Ct. App. 1995).

Gordon v. District of Columbia, 480 F. Supp.2d 112 (D.D.C. 2007).

Hanig v. Yorktown Central School District, 384 F. Supp.2d 710 (S.D.N.Y. 2005).

Henry v. Unified School District, 328 F. Supp.2d 1130 (D. Kan. 2004).

Hess v. Rochester School District, 396 F. Supp.2d 65 (D.N.H. 2005).

Hinson v. U.S.D. No. 500, 187 F. Supp.2d 1297 (D. Kan. 2002).

Huber v. Howard County, 849 F. Supp. 407 (D. Md. 1994).

Johnson v. Paradise Valley Unified School District, 251 F.3d 1222 (9th Cir. 2001).

Keller v. Board of Education of City of Albuquerque, 182 F.2d 1148 (D.N.M. 2001).

Kurek v. North Allegheny School District, 233 Fed. Appx. 154 (3d Cir. 2007).

Linares v. City of White Plains, 773 F. Supp. 559 (S.D.N.Y. 1991).

Maddox v. University of Tennessee, 62 F.3d 843 (6th Cir. 1995).

Martin v. Barnesville Exempted Village School District Board of Education, 209 F.3d 931 (2000).

McWright v. Alexander, 982 F.2d 222 (7th Cir. 1992).

Murphy v. United Parcel Service, 527 U.S. 516 (1999).

Mustafa v. Clark County School District, 157 F.3d 1169 (9th Cir. 1998).

Nichols v. Harford County Board of Education, 189 F. Supp.2d 325 (D. Md. 2002).

Pandazides v. Virginia Board of Education, 804 F. Supp. 794 (E.D. Va. 1992), *reversed on other grounds,* 13 F.3d 823 (4th Cir. 1994).

Pierce v. Engle, 726 F. Supp. 1231 (D. Kan. 1989).

Putkowski v. Warwick Valley Central School District, 363 F. Supp.2d 649 (S.D.N.Y. 2005).

Ramirez v. New York City Board of Education, 481 F. Supp.2d 209 (E.D.N.Y. 2007).

Ransom v. State of Arizona Board of Regents, 983 F. Supp. 895 (D. Ariz. 1997).

Redlich v. Albany Law School of Union University, 899 F. Supp. 100 (N.D.N.Y. 1995).

Rehabilitation Act, Section 504, 29 U.S.C. § 794 (2005).

Ross v. Board of Education of Prince George's County, 195 F. Supp.2d 730 (D. Md. 2002).

Santiago v. Temple University, 739 F. Supp. 974 (E.D. Pa. 1990).

Sanzo v. Uniondale Union Free School District, 381 F. Supp.2d 113 (E.D.N.Y. 2005).

School Board of Nassau County, Florida v. Arline, 480 U.S. 273 (1987).

Sirota v. New York City Board of Education, 725 N.Y.S.2d 332 (N.Y. App. Div. 2001).

Smaw v. Commonwealth of Virginia Department of State Police, 862 F. Supp. 1469 (E.D. Va. 1994).

Southeastern Community College v. Davis, 442 U.S. 397 (1979).

Spells v. Cuyahoga Community College, 889 F. Supp. 1023 (N.D. Ohio 1994).

Stewart v. Weast, 228 F. Supp.2d (D. Md. 2002).

Stockton v. World of Hope Daycare, 484 F. Supp.2d 1304 (S.D. Ga. 2007).

Sullivan v. River Valley School District, 197 F.3d 804 (6th Cir. 1999), *certiorari denied*, 530 U.S. 1262 (2000).

Sutton v. United Air Lines, 527 U.S. 471 (1999).

Temple v. Board of Education of City of New York, 322 F. Supp.2d 277 (E.D.N.Y. 2004).

Toyota Motor Manufacturing v. Williams, 534 U.S. 184 (2002).

Treiber v. Lindbergh School District, 199 F. Supp.2d 949 (E.D. Mo. 2002).

Walders v. Garrett, 765 F. Supp. 303 (E.D. Va. 1991).

Wellington v. Lyon County School District, 187 F.3d 1150 (9th Cir. 1999).

Wilber v. Brady, 780 F. Supp. 837 (D.D.C. 1992).

Wilson v. Wenatchee School District, 40 P.3d 686 (Wash. Ct. App. 2002).

Winston v. Maine Technical College System, 631 A.2d 70 (Me. 1993).

Winters v. Pasadena Independent School District, 1124 Fed. Appx. 822 (5th Cir. 2005).

Wood v. Omaha School District, 25 F.3d 667 (8th Cir. 1994).

Young v. Central Square Central School District, 213 F. Supp.2d 202 (N.D.N.Y. 2002).

5 Parents and the General Public

KEY CONCEPTS IN THIS CHAPTER

❖ Pertinent Provisions of Section 504 and the ADA

❖ Application of Section 504 and the ADA to Public Entities

❖ Application of Section 504 and the ADA to Places of Public Accommodation

❖ Application of Section 504 and the ADA to Private Institutions

❖ Rights of Parents Who Have Disabilities

❖ Rights of Others Who Have Disabilities

INTRODUCTION

Students and employees are not the only ones who have access to schools or their programs. Parents and family members need access to school buildings in order to work cooperatively with educators regarding educational programming for their children. Further, as public buildings, schools also frequently provide access to the general public. In fact, many school systems offer adult education programs and other civic programs for communities-at-large so that they can gather for their own meetings and programs. In addition, individuals in a variety of service industries, such as delivery personnel, often have occasion to enter school facilities as members of the general public.

Insofar as public access to school buildings, property, and programs is common, officials in educational entities must provide the protections of

Section 504 of the Rehabilitation Act (Section 504, 2005) and the Americans With Disabilities Act (ADA, 2005) to many individuals in addition to their own students and employees. Accordingly, any benefits or services provided to the general public must be made available to parents and citizens with disabilities. In this respect, educational officials may need to provide reasonable accommodations to those outside of their school communities who may desire access to their facilities and programs. After reviewing the applicability of Section 504 and the ADA to these issues, the chapter rounds out with a summary and recommendations for educational leaders.

APPLICABLE PROVISIONS OF SECTION 504 AND THE ADA

When it comes to providing access to school property and programs to the general public, school officials may not discriminate against individuals with disabilities solely on the basis of their impairments. The definition of a disability is the same whether the individuals are students, school employees, or citizens-at-large. Further, the requirement that individuals with disabilities must be otherwise qualified to participate in the benefits offered by public educational entities with reasonable accommodations applies to the general public just as it does for students and employees.

Title II of the ADA has particular applicability to entities that allow public access, such as schools and institutions of higher learning. Title II concerns state and local governments, both as employers and as providers of public services, including transportation. Title II of the ADA is divided into two subtitles. Subtitle A, the briefer portion of the statute, prohibits discrimination against otherwise qualified individuals with disabilities by public entities such as state or local governments and their departments. Subtitle B, on the other hand, which deals with actions applicable to public transportation provided by public entities, is not directly applicable to the discussion in this chapter.

> Title II of the ADA has particular applicability to entities that allow public access, such as schools and institutions of higher learning.

Public Entities

According to Subtitle A of Title II of the ADA, no qualified individual shall "be excluded from participation in or be denied the benefits of the services, programs, or activities of a public entity" (42 U.S.C. § 12132). As such, this Subtitle is even more far reaching than either Section 504 or Title I of the ADA (which addresses employment in the private sector), because public schools and colleges fit under the all-inclusive term of a "public entity." Even though Subtitle A does not target public schools and colleges explicitly, it calls for the provision of reasonable accommodations in all programs in public schools and colleges. To this end, Subtitle A affords the federal government the authority to compel public schools and institutions of higher learning to open their programs to individuals with disabilities (Miles, Russo, & Gordon, 1991).

Public Accommodations

Title III of the ADA, which specifically prohibits discrimination by public accommodations, applies to private schools from the preschool level to postgraduate institutions (Zirkel, 2005). Under this Title, private schools, as public accommodations, must grant individuals with disabilities equal opportunities to participate in their benefits and services. Insofar as religious organizations are exempt from the ADA, private sectarian schools do not need to adhere to its requirements (*White v. Denver Seminary,* 2001).

Private Institutions

Section 504 may also apply to many private educational institutions, because most receive federal funding of some sort. One noneducation case that was decided prior to the enactment of the ADA provides an example of how far reaching the "recipients of federal funds" designation may be considered. Plaintiffs filed suit alleging that a sports stadium failed to meet federal and state accessibility requirements. City officials responded that since no public funds were used in the construction of the stadium, Section 504 was inapplicable. A federal trial court in Florida disagreed, finding that Section 504 did apply, because the city used federal block grant funds to acquire land, relocate occupants, and demolish portions of the site (*Locascio v. City of St. Petersburg,* 1990).

The Supreme Court, in a fairly recent highly publicized controversy, reviewed a dispute wherein a golfer with a circulatory leg disorder that limited his ability to walk sued a professional not-for-profit golf association over his request that he be allowed to ride a cart during events. The Court explained that since golf courses are places of public accommodations, the golfer was entitled to what amounted to a reasonable accommodation under the ADA, because he was otherwise qualified to participate in tournaments (*PGA Tour v. Martin,* 2001).

PARENTS

Parents frequently require access to schools so that they may be involved in the educational experiences of their children. For example, parents need to attend award ceremonies, athletic events, concerts, plays, graduations, and conferences with their children's teachers. Under Section 504 and the ADA, school officials are required to provide parents with reasonable accommodations so that they may be able to meaningfully participate in events that are integral to their children's educational programs.

The Second Circuit affirmed that a school board in New York was required to provide a sign-language interpreter so that parents who were hearing impaired could participate in school-initiated conferences incident to the academic and disciplinary aspects of their child's educational program (*Rothschild v. Grottenthaler* [*Rothschild*], 1989, 1990). The controversy arose when the parents, whose children were not hearing impaired, requested that school officials provide them with a sign-language interpreter so that they could participate in conferences with the teachers who instructed

> Under Section 504 and the ADA, school officials are required to provide parents with reasonable accommodations so that they may be able to meaningfully participate in events that are integral to their children's educational programs.

their children. A federal trial court determined that the parents were otherwise qualified and were entitled to meaningful access to school-initiated conferences. The court pointed out that meaningful access required officials to do more than accommodate the privately obtained interpreter. In explaining that school board officials had to take affirmative actions under the circumstances, the court ordered them to provide the requested interpreter not only for teacher conferences but also for graduation ceremonies.

On appeal, the Second Circuit observed that since the parents were interested in attending school-related functions concerning their children, they were otherwise qualified for parent-oriented activities that the school offered. Insofar as it thought that they would have been unable to participate in the activities due to their inability to communicate effectively, the court was of the view that board officials unfairly excluded the parents from participation solely because of their disabilities, in violation of Section 504. The court noted that the parents were not excluded from the protections of Section 504 simply because they were parents and not students. From the Second Circuit's perspective, the trial court's decision provided a reasonable accommodation in that it permitted the parents to be involved in their children's educations without overburdening the school system. Nevertheless, the appellate panel vacated that portion of the trial court's order requiring school board officials to provide an interpreter for graduation ceremonies.

Under *Rothschild*, Section 504 did not require educational officials to provide accommodations for other school functions in which parental participation is not necessary, such as school plays or even graduation ceremonies. However, since schools and their facilities, such as athletic fields and stadiums, are places of public accommodation, the result in *Rothschild* most likely would have been different under the ADA to the extent that officials would probably have been required to make the requested accommodations.

GENERAL PUBLIC

Providing physical access to buildings is one of the basic tenets of both Section 504 and the ADA. Although public entities are not required to make all parts of existing buildings accessible, they are required to do so in new construction and whenever they make alterations to existing facilities (28 C.F.R. §§ 35.150, 35.151). To this end, officials in public educational institutions should remove architectural barriers that can be easily eliminated. Moreover, institutions that provide access to the general public should undertake efforts to ensure that individuals with disabilities have the same physical access. Such access includes scheduling community and civic programs in buildings that are accessible rather than in buildings that may present obstacles to access by persons with disabilities.

A dispute that was litigated in a federal trial court in Pennsylvania demonstrates that alterations to physical plants do not need to be extensive before steps must be taken to provide access. The ADA requires curb ramps on all newly constructed or altered streets (28 C.F.R. § 35.151(e)). The court acknowledged that under the statute's regulations, resurfacing a street was an alteration that required the

> Officials in public educational institutions should remove architectural barriers that can be easily eliminated.

installation of curb ramps (*Kinney v. Yerusalim*, 1993). Consequently, public entities could be required to install curb ramps and other means of physical access to their buildings whenever they undertake a project such as repaving a parking lot or entrance, rebuilding sidewalks, or replacing curbs.

Of particular concern to private schools and institutes of higher education is the fact that dormitories need to be made accessible. In one case, the Third Circuit commented that since the ADA's regulations define dormitories as transient lodgings, any construction or alterations to student housing must comply with its provisions (*Regents of Mercersburg College v. Republic Franklin Insurance Co.*, 2006). The court added that student housing is an integral part of a boarding school, because it is one of the facilities, privileges, advantages, and accommodations of a place of education covered by the ADA.

Beyond physical access, officials in public entities must provide individuals with disabilities with opportunities to participate in the same types of programs as those that are provided to the general public. In one such case, a federal trial court in Florida found that a city violated the ADA when officials completely eliminated recreation programs for individuals with disabilities due to fiscal constraints (*Concerned Parents to Save Dreher Park Center v. City of West Palm Beach*, 1994). The court maintained that when public entities provide programs, they must use methods and criteria that do not have the purpose or effect of impairing the ADA's objectives with respect to individuals with disabilities. The court recognized that completely eliminating programs for individuals with disabilities would have had just this effect. The court noted that the ADA contemplates that different or separate benefits or services may be provided if they are necessary to give qualified individuals with disabilities aids, benefits, or services that are as effective as those provided to others. Still, the court asserted that any benefits provided to the general public must be made equally available to persons with disabilities. In the court's view, if the city chose to provide recreation services to the general public, it needed to provide equal opportunities to persons with disabilities to receive comparable benefits.

> Beyond physical access, officials in public entities must provide individuals with disabilities with similar opportunities to participate in the types of programs that are provided to the general public.

An early case illustrates the fact that individuals with disabilities are entitled to access community programs. A suit was filed on behalf of developmentally disabled individuals at state operated facilities (*Jackson v. Fort Stanton Hospital and Training School,* 1990). Evidence indicated that several residents of the facility would have benefited from placements in community programs but were denied access to those programs. The court ruled that otherwise qualified residents were entitled to be given meaningful access to community programs operated by the state, even if reasonable accommodations needed to be made to ensure that meaningful access. This case stands for the proposition that in similar circumstances school officials would have to make community programs that are available to the general public available to individuals with disabilities. To bar such individuals from community programs offered by a school district solely on the basis of their disabilities would be a blatant violation of Section 504 and the ADA.

Accommodations required of public entities to provide individuals with disabilities with access to their benefits must be reasonable. The standard in this respect is the same as it is for the accommodations that must be provided to students and employees. Any accommodations that are excessively costly, create an undue administrative burden, or cause institutions to alter their missions substantially are not required. In this respect the federal trial court in Minnesota refused to require a day care center to provide one-on-one child care to a developmentally delayed child (*Roberts v. Kindercare Learning Centers, Inc.,* 1995). Finding that such a requirement would fundamentally alter the nature of the day care center's services, the court specified that it would have necessitated center officials to expend nearly double the tuition fee that they received to provide this service. The court concluded that such an approach was unnecessary, because it would have imposed an undue financial and administrative burden on the center.

SUMMARY

As both recipients of federal funds and as places of public accommodation, almost all schools and institutions of higher education come under the auspices of Section 504 and the ADA. Educational officials in schools and other educational institutions must provide reasonable accommodations so that otherwise qualified parents and individuals may have meaningful access to the programs, services, and benefits that they offer. The definition of a disability remains essentially the same whether the individual is a student, employee, parent, or citizen-at-large. By the same token, the requirements and guidelines for providing reasonable accommodations are similar.

First and foremost, officials in all educational institutions should remove any architectural barriers that would prevent physical access to facilities. Although the antidiscrimination statutes do not require extensive renovations to existing facilities, artificial barriers that would prevent physical access by an individual with disabilities should be removed. In other words, even though institutions may not be required to install elevators in existing buildings, it would be prudent to undertake such minor renovations as installing curb cuts, building wheelchair ramps, widening doors, and providing appropriate seating in public areas.

At the same time, meaningful access requires more than providing physical access. Many parents and members of the general public who have disabilities require accommodations so that they may participate in programs and benefits to the same extent as their peers who do not have disabilities. In this respect, officials in educational institutions need to take whatever steps are necessary to ensure that individuals with disabilities are able to participate fully in offerings. Again, as with the accommodations that must be provided to students and employees, the accommodations provided to others must be reasonable. In this respect, accommodations that are unduly expensive, create administrative burdens, or cause entities to alter their basic mission are not likely to be considered reasonable.

Additionally, requested accommodations must have a direct relationship to the individual's disability and must be required as a result of the person's impairment. Figure 5.1 addresses some frequently asked questions about the application of Section 504 and the ADA to parents and the general public.

RECOMMENDATIONS FOR PRACTICE

Educational leaders at all levels should

- conduct frequent Section 504/ADA audits of their programs and facilities to ensure that artificial barriers that could impede physical access by individuals with disabilities do not exist.
- form committees that include individuals with disabilities to advise them regarding the steps that they should take to come into full compliance with Section 504 and the ADA.
- provide accommodations to parents so that they may participate in school functions that are necessary to their children's educations; this includes events such as orientation meetings, report card conferences, and disciplinary meetings.
- consider providing accommodations for other events that are important for parents and their children; this includes meetings of the parent-teacher organization, performances, and curriculum-related events such as science fairs.
- note that a lack of funds is not a defense for failing to provide equal access; if programs, services, and benefits are provided to those who do not have disabilities, equivalent programs, services, and benefits must be provided to those who do have disabilities.
- examine their community use policies to make sure that provisions are made for individuals with disabilities.

Figure 5.1   Frequently Asked Questions

Q. What are the implications of Section 504 and the ADA for school community use policies?

A. If schools open their facilities to the general public for community use, officials must not discriminate against individuals with disabilities solely because of their disabilities. Provisions need to be made so that individuals with disabilities may have meaningful access to any community use programs held in school facilities. This means that programs should meet, whenever possible, in buildings that are accessible.

Q. Do school officials have an affirmative duty to provide accommodations to parents so that they may participate in events relating to the education of their children?

A. Generally speaking, it is the responsibility of individuals with disabilities to request accommodations. However, since parental participation in school events is desirable, school officials should reach out to parents with disabilities to see what they can do to better facilitate their participation.

REFERENCES

Americans With Disabilities Act, 42 U.S.C. §§ 12101 *et seq.* (2005).

Concerned Parents to Save Dreher Park Center v. City of West Palm Beach, 846 F. Supp. 986 (S.D. Fla. 1994).

Jackson v. Fort Stanton Hospital and Training School, 757 F. Supp. 1243 (D.N.M. 1990).

Kinney v. Yerusalim, 812 F. Supp. 547 (E.D. Pa. 1993).

Locascio v. City of St. Petersburg, 731 F. Supp. 1522 (M.D. Fla. 1990).

Miles, A. S., Russo, C. J., & Gordon, W. M. (1991). The reasonable accommodations provisions of the Americans With Disabilities Act. *Education Law Reporter, 69,* 1–8.

PGA Tour v. Martin, 532 U.S. 661 (2001).

Regents of Mercersburg College v. Republic Franklin Insurance Co., 458 F.3d 159 (3d Cir. 2006).

Rehabilitation Act, Section 504, 29 U.S.C. § 794 (2005).

Roberts v. Kindercare Learning Centers, Inc., 896 F. Supp. 921 (D. Minn. 1995).

Rothschild v. Grottenthaler, 716 F. Supp. 796 (S.D.N.Y. 1989), 725 F. Supp. 776 (S.D.N.Y. 1989), *affirmed in part, vacated and remanded in part,* 907 F.2d 286 (2d Cir. 1990).

White v. Denver Seminary, 157 F. Supp.2d 1171 (D. Colo. 2001).

Zirkel, P.A. (2005). *Section 504, the ADA and the schools* (2nd ed., Supp. 4). Horsham, PA: LRP Publications.

6 Defenses, Immunities, and Remedies

INTRODUCTION

When recipients of federal financial assistance are found to have violated Section 504 of the Rehabilitation Act (Section 504, 2005) or the Americans With Disabilities Act (ADA, 2005), courts frequently order prospective relief. In other words, courts often order officials in public educational institutions to take corrective measures. However, in some circumstances, courts also order compensatory remedies to make up for past wrongs.

This chapter reviews a variety of topics associated with the options that courts have in evaluating whether discrimination claims that are filed against public educational institutions under Section 504 and the ADA have merit. More specifically, the chapter begins by addressing defenses that educational institutions may rely on, the sovereign immunity of states and state agencies, and damages awards. The chapter next reviews whether officials may be sued in their individual capacities, statutes of limitations for filing suits, and attorney fee awards for successful plaintiffs. Then, due to the interrelationship of Section 504 and the ADA to the Individuals with Disabilities Education Act (IDEA, 2005) for students in elementary and secondary schools, the chapter examines the requirement that aggrieved parties first pursue remedies under the latter act before filing suits under the former statutes. Following a review of these materials, the chapter concludes with a summary and recommendations for educational leaders.

DEFENSES

Education officials can rely on one of three defenses to avoid being charged with noncompliance with Section 504 or the ADA even when individuals appear to be otherwise qualified. These defenses emerged largely as a result of two Supreme Court cases filed under Section 504, *Southeastern Community College v. Davis* (*Davis*, 1979) and *School Board of Nassau County, Florida v. Arline* (*Arline*, 1987).

In *Davis* the Supreme Court held that officials at a community college did not violate the rights of an unsuccessful applicant to a nursing program. The Court was convinced that since officials denied the applicant's entry into the program because her hearing impairment would have made it unsafe for her to participate, she was not otherwise qualified to participate. Conversely, in *Arline,* the Court acknowledged that school officials violated a teacher's rights by discharging her due to recurrences of tuberculosis. In remanding the case to the federal trial court for a consideration of whether the teacher was otherwise qualified for the job, the Court borrowed language from an *amicus curiae* or friend of the court brief filed by the American Medical Association to create a four-part test for use in cases involving contagious diseases. The factors that the Court instructed the lower court to examine on remand were the nature of the risk, its duration, its severity, and the probabilities that the disease would be transmitted and cause varying degrees of harm. On remand, a federal trial court in Florida reasoned that since the teacher was otherwise qualified, she was entitled to return to her job (*Arline v. School Board of Nassau County*, 1988).

Educational institutions may rely on a number of defenses against suits filed by individuals with disabilities under Section 504 and the ADA. The first defense is that education officials can be excused from making accommodations that result either in "a fundamental alteration in the nature of [a] program" (*Southeastern Community College v. Davis*, 1979, p. 410). The second defense permits school officials to avoid reasonable accommodations if modifications impose an "undue financial burden" (*Davis,* p. 412) on institutions or entities as a whole. The third defense is that otherwise qualified individuals with disabilities can be excluded from programs if their presence creates a substantial risk of injury to themselves or others (*School Board of Nassau County, Florida v. Arline*, 1987). For example, under this defense, children with severe visual impairments could be excluded from using scalpels in biology laboratories. On the other hand, in seeking to comply with Section 504 and the ADA, school personnel would most likely have to offer reasonable accommodations, such as supplying a computer-assisted program to achieve an instructional goal similar to the one that would have been achieved in a standard laboratory class.

> Educational institutions may rely on a number of defenses against suits filed by individuals with disabilities under Section 504 and the ADA.

As a final point, Section 504, which is enforced by the Office of Civil Rights, requires recipients of federal financial aid to file assurances of compliance; provide notice to students and their parents that their programs are nondiscriminatory; engage in remedial actions where violations are proven; take voluntary steps to overcome the effects of conditions that resulted in limiting the participation of students with disabilities in their programs; conduct self-evaluations; designate a staff member, typically at the central office level, as compliance coordinator; and adopt grievance procedures (34 C.F.R. § 104.5). The ADA's regulations contain similar requirements (28 C.F.R. §§ 35.105–35.107).

ELEVENTH AMENDMENT IMMUNITY

The Eleventh Amendment to the U.S. Constitution provides the states with immunity from suits in federal courts. Even so, Congress can abrogate the states' sovereign immunity when it enacts legislation (Osborne, 1990). In 1985 the U.S. Supreme Court, in *Atascadero State Hospital v. Scanlon* (*Atascadero*, 1985), a noneducation case, emphatically ruled that Congress may abrogate the states' Eleventh Amendment immunity when it enacts legislation if it makes its intention to do so known in clear and unmistakable language within the statute itself.

Acting in response to *Atascadero*, Congress amended Title VI of the Civil Rights Act (2005) to clarify that states are not immune to suits in federal courts filed under several civil rights statutes, including Section 504 (42 U.S.C. § 2000d-7). Similarly, Congress included a statement in the ADA indicating that states were not immune to actions filed under its provisions (42 U.S.C. § 12202). In spite of this, controversy has existed over whether states and state agencies can use the Eleventh Amendment as a defense in suits filed under Section 504 and the ADA. Although there are some exceptions, most courts agree that by accepting federal funds, states waive their Eleventh Amendment immunity for Section 504 purposes. It is now fairly well settled that Congress did not validly abrogate the states' sovereign immunity under Title I of the ADA, but whether it did so for Title II in the context of education is still uncertain.

> Controversy has existed over whether states and state agencies can use the Eleventh Amendment as a defense in suits filed under these laws.

Sovereign Immunity Under Section 504

The issue of whether states are immune from suits under Section 504 has resulted in mixed judicial opinions. Still, most courts agree that states do not enjoy Eleventh Amendment immunity under Section 504. The First (*Nieves-Marquez v. Commonwealth of Puerto Rico*, 2003), Third (*A. W. v. Jersey City Public Schools*, 2003), Fifth (*Bennett-Nelson v. Louisiana Board of Regents*, 2005; *Miller v. Texas Tech University Health Sciences Center*, 2005; *Pace v. Bogalusa City School Board*, 2005), Sixth (*Carten v. Kent State University*, 2002), Eighth (*Jim C. v. United States*, 2000), and Tenth (*Robinson v. Kansas*, 2002) Circuits have ruled that Puerto Rico, New Jersey, Louisiana, Texas, Ohio, Arkansas, and Kansas, respectively, waived their immunity under Section 504 by accepting federal funds. In addition, federal trial courts in Colorado (*Werner v. Colorado State University*, 2000), Hawaii (*Patricia N. v. LeMahieu*, 2001; *Patrick and Kathy W. v. LeMahieu*, 2001), and Virginia (*Shepard v. Irving*, 2002) have declared that those states waived their immunity for similar reasons.

Conversely, on remand from the Supreme Court, the Eleventh Circuit affirmed that suits in federal court by state employees to recover money damages under Section 504 are barred by the Eleventh Amendment (*Garrett v. University of Alabama at Birmingham*, 2001). Similarly, the federal trial court in Maryland decided that a school board, as a state agency, was immune from litigation filed on the basis of Section 504 (*Biggs v. Board of Education of Cecil County*, 2002).

Sovereign Immunity Under the ADA

In one of the first cases to address the question of Eleventh Amendment immunity under the ADA, the Eleventh Circuit declared that the statute included a clear statement of Congressional intent to abrogate the states' sovereign immunity (*Kimel v. State of Florida Board of Regents,* 1998). In a subsequent case from Alabama, that same court reversed a lower court's dismissal on Eleventh Amendment grounds of a damages suit filed by two state employees who alleged that they were subjected to discriminatory treatment under the ADA (*Garrett v. University of Alabama at Birmingham Board of Trustees,* 1999). As noted above, the Supreme Court (*Garrett v. University of Alabama at Birmingham,* 2001) affirmed and, on remand, in relevant part, the Eleventh Circuit agreed (*Garrett v. University of Alabama at Birmingham,* 2001).

Following the Tenth Circuit's precedent (*Martin v. Kansas,* 1999), a federal trial court in Colorado also noted that the ADA abrogated Eleventh Amendment immunity (*Werner v. Colorado State University,* 2000).

Against that backdrop, in 2001, the U.S. Supreme Court reversed the Eleventh Circuit's decision in the dispute from Alabama. In *Board of Trustees of the University of Alabama v. Garrett* (*Garrett,* 2001), the Court decided that in order to authorize private individuals to recover money damages, there must be a pattern of discrimination by the states that violates the Fourteenth Amendment, and the remedy imposed by Congress must be congruent and proportional to the violation. Insofar as the Court did not think that these requirements were met when Congress passed Title I of the ADA, it reversed the Eleventh Circuit's judgment. On remand, the Eleventh Circuit affirmed that Eleventh Amendment immunity bars suits in federal court by state employees to recover money damages by reason of a state's failure to comply with the ADA (*Garrett v. University of Alabama at Birmingham,* 2001).

Shortly after *Garrett* was handed down, the federal trial court in Puerto Rico maintained that the Eleventh Amendment barred ADA suits in federal courts for monetary damages unless the jurisdictions being sued waived their immunity or consented to subjecting themselves to litigation (*Vizcarrondo v. Board of Trustees of the University of Puerto Rico,* 2001). Similarly, when a student filed suit in Arkansas, a federal trial court followed *Garrett* by declaring that Congress did not validly abrogate the states' Eleventh Amendment immunity from suits for money damages under Title I (*Doe v. Barger,* 2002). A year later, citing *Garrett,* a federal trial court in Virginia dismissed an employee's claim against a state college for monetary damages (*Allen v. College of William and Mary,* 2003).

To the extent that *Garrett* involved Title I of the ADA, which prohibits employment discrimination, it does not specifically apply to Title II of the ADA, which prohibits discrimination in services, programs, or activities of public entities. In 2004 the Supreme Court, in another noneducation case, *Tennessee v. Lane* (*Lane*, 2004), addressed the issue of immunity under Title II. This controversy began when two paraplegics filed suit alleging that officials of the state of Tennessee and specified counties within it denied them physical access to state courts in violation of Title II of the ADA. The federal trial court denied the state's motion to dismiss pursuant to the Eleventh Amendment. On further review, the Sixth Circuit affirmed that the plaintiffs' claims were not barred, because they were based on due process principles. The Supreme Court affirmed in essentially asserting that as it applied to cases implicating the fundamental right of access to the courts, Title II constituted a valid exercise of Congress' authority to enforce the Fourteenth Amendment's substantive guarantees. The Court observed that Title II was an appropriate response to Congress's determination that there was an extensive history and pattern of unequal treatment in areas such as access to public services. Further, the Court commented that Title II's requirement of program accessibility is congruent and proportional to its object of enforcing the right of access to the courts.

It is important to note that in *Lane* the Supreme Court limited its opinion to the situation before it, namely access to the courts. Accordingly, *Lane* does not automatically apply to issues of access to educational programs, because the services that schools provide are not necessarily equivalent to those of courts. Prior to the Court's pronouncement in *Lane*, most lower courts agreed that the Eleventh Amendment protected states from claims brought on the basis of Title II in an educational context. For example, on two occasions the Sixth Circuit, following its own precedent (*Popovich v. Cuyahoga County Court of Common Pleas*, 2002) indicated that the Eleventh Amendment barred equal protection ADA Title II claims against state educational institutions (*Carten v. Kent State University*, 2002; *Robinson v. University of Akron School of Law*, 2002).

The education cases decided after *Lane* provide two distinct interpretations. How courts are likely to resolve whether states are entitled to Eleventh Amendment immunity under Title II may well depend on how they view the right to education. While the Supreme Court made it clear that education is not a fundamental right under the U.S. Constitution (*San Antonio Independent School District v. Rodriguez*, 1973), many state courts have interpreted their state constitutions as making it such a right, because it is vital to the well being of society. Further, courts may distinguish between higher education and elementary and secondary education in that students' rights to elementary and secondary education are closer to being fundamental than is the right to a higher education.

Other federal trial courts have kept a state's sovereign immunity to suits under Title II intact. A federal trial court in New York refused to expand the scope of Title II by encroaching on the state's immunity with respect to the right to education, a right that it considered to be nonfundamental (*Press v. State University of New York at Stony Brook*, 2005). Similarly, the federal trial court in Connecticut declared that since the right to an education is neither explicitly nor implicitly guaranteed in the Constitution, it is not fundamental (*Johnson v. Southern Connecticut State University*, 2004). Moreover, the court noted that the dispute arose in the context of higher education and that there was no fundamental right to higher education. The federal trial court in Maryland, with little explanation, wrote that since education has not been identified as a fundamental right, the Eleventh Amendment remains intact for education claims under Title II (*McNulty v. Board of Education of Calvert County*, 2004). However, a year later, the Fourth Circuit, in a decision that is discussed in the next paragraph, reached the opposite result (*Constantine v. Rectors and Visitors of George Mason University*, 2005).

On the flip side, the First, Fourth, and Eleventh Circuits agreed that Congress validly abrogated Eleventh Amendment immunity in regard to Title II. The First Circuit proclaimed that the ADA's prophylactic measures were justified by the persistent pattern of exclusion and irrational treatment of students with disabilities in public education (*Toledo v. Sanchez*, 2006). Concluding that Title II did, in fact, constitute a valid exercise of Congress' authority to enforce the guarantees of the Fourteenth Amendment, the court noted that Title II created an affirmative obligation on states to reasonably modify their programs to accommodate otherwise qualified students with disabilities. The Fourth Circuit affirmed that it could not find that Title II was so out of proportion to a supposed remedial or preventive object that it could not be understood to be responsive to, or designed to prevent, unconstitutional behavior (*Constantine v. Rectors and Visitors of George Mason University*, 2005). Thus, the court asserted that Title II was valid Fourteenth Amendment legislation at least as it applied to public higher education. The Eleventh Circuit, although positing that education was not a fundamental right, acknowledged that it was vital to the future success of American society (*Association for Disabled Americans v. Florida International University*, 2005). Insofar as discrimination against individuals with disabilities affects their future ability to exercise and participate in the most basic rights and responsibilities of citizenship, the court insisted that the relief available under Title II was congruent and proportional to the injury and the means adopted to remedy the injury.

Effect on State Agencies and School Boards

Most courts have concurred that state agencies, as arms of the state, are also immune from suits under the ADA if their respective states are immune. The federal trial court in Puerto Rico conceded that as an instrumentality of the Commonwealth, the University of Puerto Rico was protected from suits in federal courts by the Eleventh Amendment (*Vizcarrondo v. Board of Trustees of the University of Puerto Rico*, 2001). Similarly, a federal trial court in Florida thought that a university was an arm of the state entitled to sovereign immunity (*Association for Disabled Americans v. Florida International University*, 2001). Although that decision was later reversed on other grounds, the point that a state college is a state agency is still valid.

Insofar as education is a function of the states, local school boards may be entitled to sovereign immunity to the same extent that the state would be immune. For example, on at least two occasions the federal trial court in Maryland granted a school board's motion to dismiss a suit on the ground of the Eleventh Amendment, insisting that it was a state agency (*Biggs v. Board of Education of Cecil County*, 2002; *McNulty v. Board of Education of Calvert County*, 2004).

DAMAGES

Generally speaking, the relief granted when courts determine that officials in educational institutions violated Section 504 or the ADA is prospective. In other words, courts usually order officials to take corrective action and not make the same mistake in the future. In employment contexts, plaintiffs who were inappropriately dismissed may be entitled to back wages (*Casino v. Mahopac Central School District*, 1989; *Doe v. District of Columbia*, 1992). Nevertheless, some plaintiffs have sought compensatory damages along with prospective remedies. Yet, it should be kept in mind that claims for monetary damages cannot be maintained against entities that enjoy Eleventh Amendment immunity. In educational contexts, this particularly applies to cases filed under Title I of the ADA. As the discussion in the previous section indicated, courts reach mixed results on the issue of sovereign immunity under Title II of the ADA.

Schools and other educational facilities are not liable for compensatory damages as long as school officials did not act in bad faith, show gross misjudgment, or discriminate intentionally against individuals with disabilities (*Finn ex rel. Stephen P. v. Harrison Central School District*, 2007; *Sellers v. School Board of the City of Manassas*, 1997, 1998; *Wenger v. Canastota Central School District*, 1997). For example, the Eighth Circuit decided that parents who failed to show that state education officials acted in bad faith or with gross misjudgment were not entitled to damages (*Bradley v. Arkansas Department of Education*, 2002). Other courts have found that in order to be entitled to compensatory damages under Section 504 or the ADA, plaintiffs must prove that defendants engaged in intentional discrimination (*Swenson v. Lincoln County School District No. 2*, 2003; *Wood v. President and Trustees of Spring Hill College*, 1992). Even though plaintiffs may allege that school officials knowingly discriminated against them, they must prove that educators did so with discriminatory animus or ill will (*Garcia v. S.U.N.Y. Health Sciences Center of Brooklyn*, 2001; *Hamilton v. City College of the City University of New York*, 2001).

> Schools and other educational facilities are not liable for compensatory damages as long as school officials did not act in bad faith, show gross misjudgment, or discriminate intentionally against individuals with disabilities.

On the other hand, the Third (*W. B. v. Matula*, 1995) and Eighth (*Rodgers v. Magnet Cove Public Schools*, 1994) Circuits specifically pointed out that Section 504 did not preclude awards of monetary damages. A federal trial court in Florida also posited that damages were available under Section 504 for intentional discrimination or retaliatory conduct when plaintiffs attempt to assert their rights under the statute (*Whitehead v. School Board for Hillsborough County*, 1996).

The federal trial court in Hawaii refused to dismiss a damages claim filed by parents of a child with autism (*Patricia N. v. LeMahieu*, 2001). The court was satisfied that the parents offered sufficient evidence of deliberate indifference by school officials to support their claim for damages. Similarly, a federal trial court in New York denied a school board's motion for summary judgment where parents of a child with disabilities presented evidence that school officials failed to develop appropriate educational programs for their son for several years (*Butler v. South Glens Falls Central School District*, 2000). According to the court, the parents' allegations, if proven, could have constituted deliberate indifference to the fact that officials violated the student's rights.

INDIVIDUAL DEFENDANTS

Ordinarily, plaintiffs file suits against institutions such as school boards, colleges, universities, or their boards of trustees. At the same time, plaintiffs may also name individual educational leaders in their official capacities. In other words, when individuals are named in litigation, they are being sued by virtue of their official positions or capacities. For the most part, courts have not allowed suits filed against individual defendants in their personal capacities to proceed (*Bracey v. Buchanan*, 1999; *Coddington v. Adelphi University*, 1999).

In a case from Pennsylvania, a student filed a suit under Section 504 and the ADA against a faculty member alleging sexual harassment on the basis of her known mental disability. The faculty member moved to dismiss the suit, claiming that the two statutes did not apply because he was not a public entity. A federal trial court disagreed, holding that since the faculty member was being sued in his official capacity, the student's claim was properly filed against a public entity (*Doe v. Marshall*, 1995).

Individual officials may be personally liable for their actions under Section 504 or the ADA if plaintiffs can demonstrate that they acted with bad faith or with gross misjudgment that was essentially outside of the scope of their duties (*Bradley v. Arkansas Department of Education*, 2002). For example, teachers can be individually liable for egregious failures to abide by the terms of students' IEPs or Section 504 service plans (*Doe v. Withers*, 1993). Moreover, a federal trial court in Pennsylvania had no difficulty in rendering individuals liable for violations of Section 504 (*McCachren v. Blacklick Valley School District*, 2002).

> Individual officials may be personally liable for their actions under Section 504 or the ADA if plaintiffs can demonstrate that they acted with bad faith or with gross misjudgment that was essentially outside of the scope of their duties.

ATTORNEY FEES

Individuals who prevail in suits alleging violations of either Section 504 or the ADA may recover their legal costs in pursuing their claims. Section 504 allows courts to award attorney fees and other legal costs to successful plaintiffs in actions or proceedings to enforce or charge violations of its provisions (29 U.S.C. § 794a(b)). The ADA contains a similar provision (42 U.S.C. § 12205).

Courts generally grant requests for attorney fees to claimants who achieved all or most of the objectives that they sought in litigation (*Carr v. Fort Morgan School District*, 1998). In order to be eligible to receive awards of attorney fees, applicants must be able to demonstrate that their cases contributed significantly to obtaining the relief that they sought (*Child v. Spillane*, 1989). Courts do not award fees in situations where initial judgments favorable to plaintiffs are overturned on appeal (*Pottgen v. Missouri State High School Activities Association*, 1997).

> Individuals who prevail in suits alleging violations of either Section 504 or the ADA may recover their legal costs in pursuing their claims.

In awarding attorney fees, courts base relief on the rates generally charged in the specific locations of the jurisdiction where suits were litigated (*Guckenberger v. Boston University*, 1998). This means that it is possible that parents living in a large urban area may be entitled to larger reimbursements than those living in rural locations, since the cost of living in cities is usually greater. Moreover, even attorneys working for a nonprofit law office are compensated at the prevailing rate in the jurisdiction (*Elliott v. Board of Education of the Rochester City School District*, 2003).

Fee awards to educational institutions are rare. In order to collect fee reimbursements, educational entities must show that the actions of a plaintiff were frivolous, unreasonable, or groundless. For example, the federal trial court in Maine refused to award fees to a university that prevailed in a suit filed by a student (*Halasz v. University of New England*, 1993). The court commented that although the student lost on all of his claims, his case was not the type of meritless, unreasonable action for which attorney fees should be awarded. Similarly, the First Circuit affirmed that attorney fees could not be awarded to a prevailing defendant unless the defendant can show that the plaintiff's suit was totally unfounded, frivolous, or otherwise unreasonable under the circumstances (*Bercovitch v. Baldwin School*, 1999).

EXHAUSTION OF IDEA ADMINISTRATIVE REMEDIES

It is not unusual for students with disabilities to file suits simultaneously alleging violations of the IDEA, Section 504, and the ADA. Still, plaintiffs must exhaust all administrative remedies under the IDEA if it makes relief available before taking their complaints to state or federal courts (20 U.S.C. § 1415(1)). Although no such requirement exists under either Section 504 or the ADA (*Cheney v. Highland Community College*, 1994; *Petersen v. University of Wisconsin Board of Regents*, 1993; *Tuck v. HCA Health Services of Tennessee*, 1993), it is fairly well settled that when the IDEA provides relief, administrative remedies must be exhausted prior to resorting to the courts, even when claims are made solely under Section 504 or the ADA. To this end, plaintiffs cannot circumvent the IDEA process by filing their complaint under the disability discrimination statutes. However, if relief is available only under Section 504 or the ADA, plaintiffs are not required to exhaust administrative remedies.

> When the IDEA provides relief, administrative remedies must be exhausted prior to resorting to the courts, even when claims are made solely under Section 504 or the ADA.

Noting how Section 504 and the ADA differ from the IDEA, on at least three occasions federal trial courts in New York required parents to exhaust administrative remedies under the IDEA in deciding that the administrative process could provide them with the relief they sought (*Cave v. East Meadow Union Free School District*, 2007; *F. N. v. Board of Education of Sachem Central School District at Holbrook*, 1995; *Kielbus v. New York City*

Board of Education, 2001). In the first case, the court rejected the student's request to enjoin his suspension, since the court was satisfied that school officials had decided that since he did not have a disability, he was not entitled to special education. In the second case, the court rejected the claims of a father of a student with hearing impairments who alleged that his son was excluded from programs for which he was eligible and that his instructors were not properly qualified or trained. In the third case, parents unsuccessfully filed suit after school officials denied permission for their son to bring a service dog to school. In rejecting the parents' request for an injunction, the court explained that the situation could have been addressed through the IDEA's dispute resolution procedures. Further, in a case from Maine, the federal trial court asserted that the failure of parents who sought home-based support services to exhaust their IDEA administrative remedies was fatal to their Section 504 and IDEA claims (*Ciresoli v. M.S.A.D. No. 22,* 1995).

The Seventh Circuit also required a student in Illinois whose complaint dealt with a situation that had an educational source and adverse educational consequences to exhaust the IDEA's administrative remedies even though he was not seeking relief under that act (*Charlie F. v. Board of Education of Skokie School District 68,* 1996). The First Circuit contended that the exhaustion principle applies even when an action is brought under another statute as long as a party is seeking relief that is available under the IDEA (*Frazier v. Fairhaven School Committee,* 2000). The court thought that the administrative process facilitated the development of a full record by a fact finder versed in the educational needs of students with disabilities.

Courts do not allow plaintiffs to circumvent the IDEA's administrative process by filing suits under other statutes such as Section 504 and the ADA. For example, a federal trial court in North Carolina, noting that Congress perceived the IDEA as being the most effective vehicle for protecting the right of a student to an appropriate education, remarked that allowing a plaintiff to circumvent its administrative remedies would be inconsistent with Congress's carefully tailored scheme (*Glen III v. Charlotte-Mecklenburg Board of Education,* 1995). The court added that in a situation such as the one before it, where the IDEA was available to a student claiming a right to an appropriate education, that statute was the exclusive avenue through which he could assert the claim. Applying a similar rationale, the Supreme Court of Wyoming emphasized that if the relief sought is available under the IDEA, parties cannot deliberately avoid that act's procedures by filing claims under other laws (*Kooperman v. Fremont County School District,* 1996).

In like fashion, a federal trial court in New York decided that plaintiffs who wanted educational officials to employ specific methodologies in working with their children who had autism could not avoid the IDEA's exhaustion requirement by claiming relief that was unavailable under that act when their claims were directly related to the appropriateness of their educational placements (*BD v. DeBuono*, 2000). Another federal trial court in New York, while conceding that the IDEA is not the exclusive avenue by which parents may enforce the rights of children with disabilities, maintained that the right to pursue remedies via other statutes was conditioned on the IDEA's exhaustion requirements for claims seeking relief available under that statute (*Hope v. Cortines*, 1995). On further review, the Second Circuit affirmed the order of the trial court.

On the other hand, courts do not require plaintiffs to exhaust the IDEA's administrative remedies when claims are purely related to discrimination or the IDEA does not offer relief. For example, the Tenth Circuit did not require parents who challenged the admission practices of a military academy to use the IDEA's process, since their suit had nothing to do with the provision of an appropriate education (*Ellenburg v. New Mexico Military Institute*, 2007). A state court in Texas ruled that two students with learning disabilities, who had been denied waivers for sports participation, were not required to exhaust administrative remedies under the IDEA, because relief was available only under Section 504 inasmuch as the students were not alleging a denial of an appropriate education (*University Interscholastic League v. Buchanan*, 1993). In another similar situation, where a student with disabilities who attended a private parochial school lost his athletic eligibility, a federal trial court in Ohio maintained that the IDEA's process was unavailable to him (*Rhodes v. Ohio High School Athletic Association*, 1996).

STATUTE OF LIMITATIONS

Neither Section 504 nor the ADA contains a statute of limitations for filing suit. Limitations periods must thus be borrowed from analogous state laws. Courts in most jurisdictions have borrowed statutes of limitations from their own disability discrimination or other civil rights laws. However, other courts have appropriated limitations periods from personal injury statutes. The statute from which the limitations periods are borrowed sometimes depends on the nature of the suits themselves. Limitations periods can range anywhere from a few months to several years.

Most states have their own laws protecting the civil rights of individuals with disabilities. These laws are generally either modeled on or patterned after Section 504 and the ADA. As such, state disability statutes typically provide the ideal vehicle for borrowing a statute of limitations.

By way of illustration, the Fourth Circuit ruled that the Virginia Rights of Persons with Disabilities Act (2004) applied in the commonwealth because that act was written to be consistent with Section 504 (*J. S. ex rel. Duck v. Isle of Wight County School Board*, 2005; *Wolsky v. Medical College of Hampton Roads*, 1993). Similarly, a federal trial court in California was convinced that the state's disability statutes (California Disabled Persons Act, 1999; Unrah Civil Rights Act, 1999) were not only analogous but were virtually identical to Section 504 and the ADA. Consequently, the court adopted the three-year statute of limitations applicable to those statutes for actions arising under Section 504 and the ADA (*Kramer v. Regents of the University of California*, 1999). A federal trial court in Connecticut borrowed a three-year limitations period from that state's civil rights laws, because discrimination claims based on disability resembled other civil rights actions (*Wills v. Ferrandino*, 1993).

> Neither Section 504 nor the ADA contains a statute of limitations for filing suit. Limitations periods must thus be borrowed from analogous state laws. Courts in most jurisdictions have borrowed statutes of limitations from their own disability discrimination or other civil rights laws.

Conversely, other courts determined that state personal injury laws are more analogous to the actions arising out of Section 504 and the ADA. The Fifth Circuit was convinced that personal injury claims were most analogous to discrimination claims, because the latter were essentially claims for personal injury (*Hickey v. Irving Independent School District*, 1992). Basically, courts applying a limitations period from personal injury statutes view acts of discrimination as fundamental injuries to the individual rights of plaintiffs (*Morse v. University of Vermont*, 1992).

Generally speaking, limitations periods begin to run on the date that plaintiffs either knew or should have known that acts of discrimination occurred (*Baker v. Board of Regents of the State of Kansas*, 1991). For instance, a federal trial court in New York granted a school board's motion for dismissal in finding that a school employee's Section 504 claim accrued on the date that he learned that he was being demoted from his position as director of transportation, allegedly due to his disability. The court rejected the claim on the ground that the Section 504 dispute was controlled by the three–year statute of limitations under state law (*Putkowski v. Warwick Valley Central School District*, 2005). In a case from Virginia, the federal trial court thought that the limitations period began on the day a student graduated, because that is when her parents first learned that she would no longer receive special education services (*Richards v. Fairfax County School Board*, 1992).

The date when limitations periods begin may also be subject to state law provisions and in some cases may be tolled, or suspended, due to extenuating circumstances. A case from the Fifth Circuit is illustrative of this notion. After borrowing the limitations period from Texas's personal injury statute, the court decided that, consistent with state law, the limitations period did not begin to run until the student turned 18 (*Hickey v. Irving Independent School District*, 1992). In essence, the court tolled the limitations period during the child's minority as provided by the state statute.

SUMMARY

In defending against claims filed under either Section 504 or the ADA, educational officials may be able to rely on several possible arguments. First, officials may be able to demonstrate that individuals with disabilities were not otherwise qualified for the positions or benefits they sought. Further, educational entities are not required to provide accommodations that would fundamentally alter the nature of their programs or create undue financial burdens. Also, entities are not obligated to accommodate individuals if their presence or the modifications would present substantial risks of injury to the persons with disabilities or to others.

In some situations, the Eleventh Amendment may protect educational entities from litigation. For the most part, state agencies or arms of the state such as school boards have immunity from actions filed under Title I of the ADA. At the same time, it is fairly well settled that entities that accept federal funds have waived immunity under Section 504. Although it is still unsettled whether the same principle applies to actions filed under Title II of the ADA, most courts agree that immunity has been waived. In most situations when courts find that educational officials have violated one of the antidiscrimination laws, they order prospective relief. Even so, the door has been left open for awards of monetary damages. Moreover, courts may award attorney fees to successful plaintiffs.

Students in elementary and secondary schools who may gain relief under the IDEA must do so through its administrative due process mechanism prior to initiating judicial challenges under Section 504 or the ADA. The IDEA requires complainants to exhaust administrative remedies before seeking judicial relief. Courts have unanimously dismissed claims where plaintiffs have not done so, even in situations where they have not cited the IDEA, if they could obtain the relief sought via that act. In situations that cannot be addressed in the IDEA's administrative process, such as pure discrimination claims, courts have not required aggrieved parties to exhaust administrative remedies before initiating judicial review.

Figure 6.1 addresses some frequently asked questions about defenses, immunities, and remedies.

RECOMMENDATIONS FOR PRACTICE

School boards and educational leaders should

- make individualized determinations as to whether persons with disabilities are otherwise qualified for the benefits they are seeking.
- complete individualized inquiries as to whether requested accommodations can be reasonably provided.
- evaluate whether the Eleventh Amendment protects their institutions from litigation; this may vary according to the nature of a case and the jurisdiction where it is filed.
- consider whether relief is available under the IDEA; if it is, plaintiffs must exhaust administrative remedies under the IDEA before heading to court.
- examine the applicable statutes of limitations for their jurisdictions to ascertain whether suits have been filed within the prescribed limitations periods.

Figure 6.1   Frequently Asked Questions

Q. How are otherwise qualified individuals with disabilities defined?

A. Individuals with disabilities are otherwise qualified if they can, by relying on reasonable accommodations, meet all of a program's requirements in spite of their disabilities. For example, in employment situations, applicants for positions must be able to perform all essential job functions. In academic contexts, students must meet all requirements for entrance into or participation in programs or activities.

Q. When would requested accommodations be considered unreasonable?

A. Accommodations are unreasonable if they would require entities to make fundamental alterations to the nature of their programs, create undue financial burdens, or pose substantial risks to individuals with disabilities or others. In other words, educational institutions are not required to lower their standards, provide accommodations that are excessively expensive, or make accommodations that could cause dangerous situations to exist.

Q. Are government agencies immune from being sued in federal courts?

A. The Eleventh Amendment to the U.S. Constitution protects states, state agencies, and other arms of the state from litigation. Even so, in specified situations Congress can waive immunity when it passes legislation. Congress has done just that with regard to Section 504 and the ADA. However, the U.S. Supreme Court has ruled that Congress did not have the authority to validly waive Eleventh Amendment immunity for Title I of the ADA. Lower courts have been fairly consistent in holding that the abrogation of sovereign immunity for Section 504 is valid, and most have agreed that the waiver of immunity for Title II of the ADA is valid.

Q. When must plaintiffs use the IDEA's administrative process before seeking relief in the courts for violations of Section 504 or the ADA?

A. For the most part, exhaustion is required whenever the IDEA's process is capable of providing the sought-after relief. Most courts have required exhaustion when plaintiffs are seeking an appropriate education. Conversely, courts have not required exhaustion when claims strictly allege discrimination. In essence, courts do not want parents to circumvent the IDEA's process by filing their complaints under Section 504 and the ADA instead of the IDEA.

Q. How long after alleged acts of discrimination do individuals with disabilities have to file suit under Section 504 or the ADA?

A. The answer depends on the state in which alleged acts occurred. Although neither Section 504 nor the ADA contains limitations periods, courts are empowered to borrow them from similar state laws. Insofar as state laws vary, limitations periods differ from one state to another. To complicate matters further, courts in different jurisdictions disagree as to whether limitations periods should be borrowed from state discrimination laws or personal injury laws.

Q. When do limitations periods start?

A. Generally, limitations periods begin on the date that individuals knew or should have known that violations of Section 504 or the ADA occurred. However, limitations periods can be suspended under certain circumstances. Often in the case of minors, limitations periods do not begin to run until individuals reach the age of majority. Limitations periods could also be suspended when officials at institutions engaged in cover-up activities so that plaintiffs were unable to determine that violations occurred.

REFERENCES

Allen v. College of William and Mary, 245 F. Supp.2d 777 (E.D. Va. 2003).

Americans With Disabilities Act, 42 U.S.C. §§ 12101 *et seq.* (2005).

Arline v. School Board of Nassau County, 692 F. Supp. 1286 (M.D. Fla.1988).

Association for Disabled Americans v. Florida International University, 405 F.3d 954 (11th Cir. 2005), *reversing* 178 F. Supp.2d 1291 (S.D. Fla. 2001).

Atascadero State Hospital v. Scanlon, 473 U.S. 234 (1985).

A. W. v. Jersey City Public Schools, 341 F.3d 234 (3d Cir. 2003).

Baker v. Board of Regents of the State of Kansas, 768 F. Supp. 1439 (D. Kan. 1991).

BD v. DeBuono, 130 F. Supp.2d 401 (S.D.N.Y. 2000).

Bennett-Nelson v. Louisiana Board of Regents, 431 F.3d 448 (5th Cir. 2005).

Bercovitch v. Baldwin School, 191 F.3d 8 (1st Cir. 1999).

Biggs v. Board of Education of Cecil County, 229 F. Supp.2d 437 (D. Md. 2002).

Bracey v. Buchanan, 55 F. Supp.2d 416 (E.D. Va. 1999).

Bradley v. Arkansas Department of Education, 301 F.3d 952 (8th Cir. 2002).

Butler v. South Glens Falls Central School District, 106 F. Supp.2d 414 (N.D.N.Y. 2000).

California Disabled Persons Act, Cal. Civ. Code § 54 (West 1999).

Carr v. Fort Morgan School District, 4 F. Supp.2d 998 (D. Colo. 1998).

Carten v. Kent State University, 282 F.3d 391 (6th Cir. 2002).

Casino v. Mahopac Central School District, 741 F. Supp. 1028 (S.D.N.Y. 1989).

Cave v. East Meadow Union Free School District, 480 F. Supp.2d 610 (E.D.N.Y. 2007).

Charlie F. v. Board of Education of Skokie School District 68, 98 F.3d 989 (7th Cir. 1996).

Cheney v. Highland Community College, 15 F.3d 79 (7th Cir. 1994).

Child v. Spillane, 866 F.2d 691 (4th Cir. 1989).

Ciresoli v. M.S.A.D. No. 22, 901 F. Supp. 378 (D. Me. 1995).

Civil Rights Act, Title VI, 42 U.S.C. §§ 2000d-1–2000d-7 (2005).

Coddington v. Adelphi University, 45 F. Supp.2d 211 (E.D.N.Y. 1999).

Constantine v. Rectors and Visitors of George Mason University, 411 F.3d 474 (4th Cir. 2005).

Doe v. Barger, 193 F. Supp.2d 1112 (E.D. Ark. 2002).

Doe v. District of Columbia, 796 F. Supp. 559 (D.D.C. 1992).

Doe v. Marshall, 882 F. Supp.2d 1504 (E.D. Pa. 1995).

Doe v. Withers, Civ. No. 92-C-92, 20 IDELR 422 (W.Va. Cir. Ct. 1993).

Ellenburg v. New Mexico Military Institute, 478 F.3d 1262 (10th Cir. 2007).

Elliott v. Board of Education of the Rochester City School District, 295 F. Supp.2d 282 (W.D.N.Y. 2003).

Finn ex rel. Stephen P. v. Harrison Central School District, 473 F. Supp.2d 477 (S.D.N.Y. 2007).

F. N. v. Board of Education of Sachem Central School District at Holbrook, 894 F. Supp. 605 (E.D.N.Y. 1995).

Frazier v. Fairhaven School Committee, 276 F.3d 52 (1st Cir. 2000).

Garcia v. S.U.N.Y. Health Sciences Center of Brooklyn, 280 F.3d 98 (2d Cir. 2001).

Garrett v. University of Alabama at Birmingham Board of Trustees, 193 F.3d 1214 (11th Cir. 1999), *certiorari granted in part*, 529 U.S. 1065 (2000), *reversed*, 531 U.S. 356 (2001), *on remand*, 261 F.3d 1242 (11th Cir. 2001), *affirmed in relevant part, vacated in other part*, 276 F.3d 1227 (11th Cir. 2001).

Glen III v. Charlotte-Mecklenburg Board of Education, 903 F. Supp. 918 (W.D.N.C. 1995).

Guckenberger v. Boston University, 8 F. Supp.2d 91 (D. Mass. 1998).

Halasz v. University of New England, 821 F. Supp. 40 (D. Me. 1993).

Hamilton v. City College of the City University of New York, 173 F. Supp.2d 181 (S.D.N.Y. 2001).

Hickey v. Irving Independent School District, 976 F.2d 980 (5th Cir. 1992).

Hope v. Cortines, 872 F. Supp. 14 (E.D.N.Y. 1995), *affirmed*, 69 F.3d 687 (2d Cir. 1995).

Individuals with Disabilities Education Act, 20 U.S.C. §§ 1400 *et seq.* (2005).

Jim C. v. United States, 235 F.3d 1079 (8th Cir. 2000).

Johnson v. Southern Connecticut State University, 2004 WL 2377225 (D. Conn. 2004).

J. S. ex rel. Duck v. Isle of Wight County School Board, 402 F.3d 468 (4th Cir. 2005).

Kielbus v. New York City Board of Education, 140 F. Supp.2d 284 (E.D.N.Y. 2001).

Kimel v. State of Florida Board of Regents, 139 F.3d 1426 (11th Cir. 1998).

Kooperman v. Fremont County School District, 911 P.2d 1049 (Wyo. 1996).

Kramer v. Regents of the University of California, 81 F. Supp.2d 972 (N.D. Cal. 1999).

Martin v. Kansas, 190 F.3d 1120 (10th Cir. 1999).

McCachren v. Blacklick Valley School District, 217 F. Supp.2d 594 (W.D. Pa. 2002).

McNulty v. Board of Education of Calvert County, 2004 WL 1554401 (D. Md. 2004)

Miller v. Texas Tech University Health Sciences Center, 421 F.3d 342 (5th Cir. 2005).

Morse v. University of Vermont, 973 F.2d 122 (2d Cir. 1992).

Nieves-Marquez v. Commonwealth of Puerto Rico, 353 F.3d 108 (1st Cir. 2003).

Osborne, A. G. (1990). States' Eleventh Amendment immunity is not abrogated by the EHA. *Education Law Reporter, 56*, 1099–1106.

Pace v. Bogalusa City School Board, 403 F.3d 272 (5th Cir. 2005).

Patricia N. v. LeMahieu, 141 F. Supp.2d (D. Haw. 2001).

Patrick and Kathy W. v. LeMahieu, 165 F. Supp.2d 1144 (D. Haw. 2001).

Petersen v. University of Wisconsin Board of Regents, 818 F. Supp. 1276 (W.D. Wis. 1993).

Popovich v. Cuyahoga County Court of Common Pleas, 276 F.3d 808 (6th Cir. 2002).

Pottgen v. Missouri State High School Activities Association, 103 F.3d 720 (8th Cir. 1997).

Press v. State University of New York at Stony Brook, 388 F. Supp.2d 127 (E.D.N.Y. 2005).

Putkowski v. Warwick Valley Central School District, 363 F. Supp.2d 649 (S.D.N.Y. 2005).

Rehabilitation Act, Section 504, 29 U.S.C. § 794 (2005).

Rhodes v. Ohio High School Athletic Association, 939 F. Supp. 584 (N.D. Ohio 1996).

Richards v. Fairfax County School Board, 798 F. Supp. 338 (E.D. Va. 1992).

Robinson v. Kansas, 295 F.3d 1183 (10th Cir. 2002).

Robinson v. University of Akron School of Law, 307 F.3d 409 (6th Cir. 2002).

Rodgers v. Magnet Cove Public Schools, 34 F.3d 642 (8th Cir. 1994).

San Antonio Independent School District v. Rodriguez, 411 U.S. 1 (1973).

School Board of Nassau County v. Arline, 480 U.S. 273 (1987).

Sellers v. School Board of the City of Manassas, 960 F. Supp.2d 1006 (E.D. Va. 1997), *affirmed*, 141 F.3d 524 (4th Cir. 1998).

Shepard v. Irving, 204 F. Supp.2d 902 (E.D. Va. 2002).

Southeastern Community College v. Davis, 442 U.S. 397 (1979).

Swenson v. Lincoln County School District No. 2, 260 F. Supp.2d 1136 (D. Wyo. 2003).

Tennessee v. Lane, 541 U.S. 509 (2004).

Toledo v. Sanchez, 454 F.3d 24 (1st Cir. 2006).

Tuck v. HCA Health Services of Tennessee, 7 F.3d 465 (6th Cir. 1993).

University Interscholastic League v. Buchanan, 848 S.W.2d 298 (Tex. Ct. App. 1993).

Unrah Civil Rights Act, Cal. Civ. Code § 51 (West 1999).

Virginia Rights of Persons with Disabilities Act, codified in Virginia Code Ann., §§ 51.5–40 *et seq.* (2004).

Vizcarrondo v. Board of Trustees of the University of Puerto Rico, 139 F. Supp.2d 198 (D.P.R. 2001).

W. B. v. Matula, 67 F.3d 484 (3d Cir. 1995).

Wenger v. Canastota Central School District, 979 F. Supp. 147 (N.D.N.Y. 1997).

Werner v. Colorado State University, 135 F. Supp.2d 1137 (D. Colo. 2000).

Whitehead v. School Board for Hillsborough County, 918 F. Supp. 1515 (M.D. Fla. 1996).

Wills v. Ferrandino, 830 F. Supp. 116 (D. Conn. 1993).

Wolsky v. Medical College of Hampton Roads, 1 F.3d 222 (4th Cir. 1993).

Wood v. President and Trustees of Spring Hill College, 978 F.2d 1214 (11th Cir. 1992).

Appendix 1

USEFUL EDUCATION LAW WEB SITES

Legal Search Engines

http://washlaw.edu

This Web site contains law-related sources on the Internet.

http://www.findlaw.com

FindLaw is an Internet resource that helps to find any Web site that is law related.

http://www.alllaw.com

AllLaw is another resource for locating law-related Web sites.

http://www.law.cornell.edu

This is a Web site sponsored by Cornell Law School; it provides research and electronic publishing.

U.S. Supreme Court, Federal Courts, and Federal Government Web Sites

http://www.supremecourtus.gov

This is the official Web site of the Supreme Court of the United States.

http://supct.law.cornell.edu/supct/index.html

This Web site contains recent decisions of the Supreme Court. It also has a free e-mail publication to distribute the syllabi of the Court's decisions within hours after they are handed down.

http://thomas.loc.gov

> This Web site was prepared by the U.S. Library of Congress and has links to the Federal Court System.

http://www.uscourts.gov

> This is the U.S. federal judiciary Web site.

http://www.gpoaccess.gov/fr/index.html

> This Web site contains the *Federal Register.*

http://www.ed.gov/about/offices/list/ocr/index.html?src=mr

> This is the Web site of the Office for Civil Rights.

http://www.house.gov

> This is the U.S. House of Representatives Web site.

http://www.senate.gov

> This is the U.S. Senate Web site.

http://www.whitehouse.gov

> This is the Web site of the White House.

http://www.ed.gov

> This is the U.S. Department of Education Web site.

http://www.ed.gov/nclb/landing.jhtml?src=pb

> This Web site contains the No Child Left Behind Act.

Appendix 2

DEPARTMENT OF SPECIAL EDUCATION WEB SITES, BY STATE

Alabama: http://www.alsde.edu/html/sections/section_detail.asp?section=65&footer=sections

Alaska: http://www.eed.state.ak.us/tls/sped/

Arizona: http://www.ade.state.az.us/menus/nine.asp

Arkansas: http://arksped.k12.ar.us/

California: http://www.cde.ca.gov/sp/se/

Colorado: http://www.cde.state.co.us/cdesped/index.asp

Connecticut: http://www.state.ct.us/sde/deps/special/

Delaware: http://www.doe.state.de.us/PROGRAMS/SPECIALED/

Florida: http://www.fldoe.org/disability/

Georgia: http://www.doe.k12.ga.us/ci_exceptional.aspx

Hawaii: http://doe.k12.hi.us/specialeducation/

Idaho: http://www.sde.idaho.gov/specialeducation/

Illinois: http://www.isbe.state.il.us/spec-ed/

Indiana: http://www.isbe.net/spec-ed/

Iowa: http://www.iowa.gov/educate/content/view/574/591/

Kansas: http://www.kansped.org/

Kentucky: http://www.kde.state.ky.us/KDE/Instructional+Resources/Exceptional+Children/

Louisiana: http://www.doe.state.la.us/lde/specialp/home.html

Maine: http://maine.gov/education/speced/

Maryland: http://www.marylandpublicschools.org/MSDE/divisions/earlyinterv/

Massachusetts: http://www.doe.mass.edu/sped/

Michigan: http://www.michigan.gov/mde/0,1607,7-140-6530_6598---,00.html

Minnesota: http://education.state.mn.us/MDE/Learning_Support/Special_Education/index.html

Mississippi: http://www.mde.k12.ms.us/special_education/

Missouri: http://dese.mo.gov/divspeced/

Montana: http://www.opi.mt.gov/SpecEd/index.html

Nebraska: http://www.nde.state.ne.us/SPED/sped.html

Nevada: http://www.doe.nv.gov/SpecialEd.htm

New Hampshire: http://www.ed.state.nh.us/education/doe/organization/instruction/bose.htm

New Jersey: http://www.state.nj.us/njded/specialed/

New Mexico: http://www.ped.state.nm.us/seo/index.htm

New York: http://www.vesid.nysed.gov/specialed/home.html

North Carolina: http://www.ncpublicschools.org/ec/

North Dakota: http://www.dpi.state.nd.us/speced/index.shtm

Ohio: http://www.ode.state.oh.us/GD/Templates/Pages/ODE/ODEPrimary.aspx?page=2&TopicRelationID=967

Oklahoma: http://se.sde.state.ok.us/ses/

Oregon: http://www.ode.state.or.us/search/results/?=40

Pennsylvania: http://www.pde.state.pa.us/special_edu/site/default.asp

Rhode Island: http://www.ride.ri.gov/Special_Populations/default.aspx

South Carolina: http://www.myscschools.com/offices/ec/

South Dakota: http://doe.sd.gov/oess/specialed/index.asp

Tennessee: http://www.state.tn.us/education/speced/

Texas: http://www.tea.state.tx.us/special.ed/

U.S. Virgin Islands: http://www.usviosep.org/

Utah: http://www.usoe.k12.ut.us/sars/

Vermont: http://www.state.vt.us/educ/new/html/pgm_sped.html

Virginia: http://www.pen.k12.va.us/VDOE/sess/

Washington: http://www.k12.wa.us/SpecialEd/default.aspx

West Virginia: http://wvde.state.wv.us/ose/

Wisconsin: http://www.dpi.state.wi.us/dpi/dlsea/een/index.html

Wyoming: http://www.k12.wy.us/se.asp

Index

CORWIN PRESS

The Corwin Press logo—a raven striding across an open book—represents the union of courage and learning. Corwin Press is committed to improving education for all learners by publishing books and other professional development resources for those serving the field of PreK–12 education. By providing practical, hands-on materials, Corwin Press continues to carry out the promise of its motto: **"Helping Educators Do Their Work Better."**